# AQA GCSE (9–1)
# Maths

## Grade 1–3 Workbook

Chris Pearce

William Collins' dream of knowledge for all began with the publication of his first book in 1819.
A self-educated mill worker, he not only enriched millions of lives, but also founded a flourishing publishing house. Today, staying true to this spirit, Collins books are packed with inspiration, innovation and practical expertise. They place you at the centre of a world of possibility and give you exactly what you need to explore it.

Collins. Freedom to teach.

Published by Collins
An imprint of HarperCollins*Publishers*
The News Building
1 London Bridge Street
London
SE1 9GF

HarperCollins*Publishers*,
1st Floor, Watermarque Building,
Ringsend Road,
Dublin 4,
Ireland

Browse the complete Collins catalogue at
**www.collins.co.uk**

10 9 8 7 6 5 4

ISBN 978-0-00-832253-3

British Library Cataloguing-in-Publication Data
A catalogue record for this publication is available from the British Library.

Author: Chris Pearce
Expert reviewer: Trevor Senior
Commissioning editor: Jennifer Hall
In-house editor: Alexandra Wells
Copyeditor: Joanne Crosby
Proof reader: Julie Bond
Answer checker: Peter Batty
Cover designers: The Big Mountain Design & Creative Direction
Cover photographs: bl: Sabine Hortebusch/Shutterstock, tr: Paolo De Gasperis/Shutterstock
Typesetter and illustrator: Jouve India Private Limited
Production controller: Katharine Willard
Printed and bound by: Ashford Colour Press Ltd

The publishers gratefully acknowledge the permission granted to reproduce the copyright material in this book. Every effort has been made to trace copyright holders and to obtain their permission for the use of copyright material. The publishers will gladly receive any information enabling them to rectify any error or omission at the first opportunity.

# Contents

# How to use this book

This workbook aims to help you build your confidence and surpass your expectations in your Mathematics GCSE. It gives you plenty of practice, guidance and support in the key topics and main sections that will have the most impact when working towards grades 1–3.

These sections are colour coded: Number, Algebra, Ratio, Proportion and Rates of Change, Geometry and Measures, Probability and Statistics.

## Question grades

You can tell the grade of each question or question part by the colour of its number:

Grade 1 questions are shown as ①

Grade 2 questions are shown as ①

Grade 3 questions are shown as ①

## Use of calculators

Questions when you could use a calculator are marked with a 🖩 icon.

## Hint boxes

The 'Hint' boxes provide you with guidance as to how to approach challenging questions.

 Hint: A **common factor** of 18 and 27 is a factor of **both** numbers.

## Key words

The 'Key words' boxes highlight important terms and mathematical language that you will need to understand for your exam. Definitions are provided in the glossary at the end of the workbook.

> **Key words**
> multiple
> common multiple

## Problem solving

This section gives examples of problem solving questions. It helps to build your problem solving and communication skills.

## Checklists

At the end of each chapter, a checklist is provided that lists the key skills and knowledge that have been covered. Use it to identify what you have mastered and what you may still need to work on. By checking off each skill, you will be putting yourself in the best position to tackle your exam.

## Answers

You will find answers to all the questions in the tear out section at the back of the book. If you are working on your own you can check your answers yourself. If you are working in class your teacher may want to go through the answers with you.

# 1 Multiples, factors and primes

## 1.1 Multiples ✗

**Key words**

multiple

common multiple

**1** Here are some multiples of 5. Write down the next three.

20, 25, 30, 35, 40, ___45___ , ___50___ , ___55___

**2** Here are the first five multiples of 7. Write down the next three.

7, 14, 21, 28, 35, ___42___ , ___49___ , ___56___

**3** What is another name for the multiples of 2?

___two times table___

**4** List the first six multiples of 11.

___11 22 33 44 55 66___

**5** List all the multiples of 20 that are less than 150.

___20 40 60 80 100 120 140___

**6** List the multiples of 3 between 20 and 40.

___21 24 27 30 33 36___

**7** Find a number that is a multiple of 4 **and** a multiple of 5.

___20 4×5 5×4 =20___

**8** Look at these numbers

90   (91)   92   (93)   94   95   [96]   97   98   (99)   100

**a** Put a circle ○ around each multiple of 3.

**b** Put a square ☐ around each multiple of 4.

**c** Which number in the list is a common multiple of 3 and 4?

_____

**9 a** Write down the first six multiples of 4.

$\underline{4 \quad 8 \quad 12 \quad 16 \quad 20 \quad 24}$

**b** Write down the first six multiples of 6.

$\underline{6 \quad 12 \quad 18 \quad 24 \quad 30 \quad 36}$

**c** Write down two common multiples of 4 and 6.

$\underline{12 \quad 24}$

**10 a** Write down the first six multiples of 15.

$\underline{15 \quad 30 \quad 45 \quad 60 \quad 75 \quad 90}$

**b** Write down the first nine multiples of 10.

$\underline{10 \quad 20 \quad 30 \quad 40 \quad 50 \quad 60 \quad 70 \quad 80 \quad 90}$

**c** Write down three common multiples of 15 and 10.

$\underline{30 \quad 60 \quad 90}$

**d** Find the **smallest** common multiple of 15 and 10.

$\underline{30}$

**11** Find **five** common multiples of 2 and 3.

28
26 (30)
2  4  (6)  8  10  (12)  14  16  (18)  20  22  (24)
3  (6)  9  (12)  15  (18)  21  (24)  27  (30)

# 1.2 Factors ✗

**1**  $15 = 1 \times 15 \qquad 15 = 3 \times 5$

Use these facts to write down the four factors of 15.

_____

**2**  List all **six** factors of the number 20.

_____

**3**  Two factors of 100 are 2 and 5.

Use this fact to work out two more factors of 100.

_____

_____

**4** Here is a list of numbers.  1  2  3  4  5  6

From the list write down the factors of

**a** 8 _____

**b** 12 _____

**c** 15 _____

**d** 17 _____

**5** **a** Write down the six factors of 18.

_____

_____

**b** Write down the four factors of 27.

_____

_____

**c** Write down the **common factors** of 18 and 27.

_____

> Hint: A **common factor** of 18 and 27 is a factor of **both** numbers.

**6** **a** Write down the five factors of 16.

_____

_____

**b** Write down the six factors of 28.

_____

_____

**c** Write down the common factors of 16 and 28.

_____

**7** Find **three** common factors of 20 and 50.

_____

_____

**8** 121 has three factors. Two of them are 1 and 121. Find the other factor.

_____

# 1.3 Prime numbers

**Key word**

prime

**1** Here is a list of numbers

10    11    12    13    14    15    16    17    18    19    20

**a** Cross out the multiples of 2.

**b** Put a circle around the prime numbers.

> Hint: A **prime** number has just two factors, e.g. 7 and 31 are prime.

**2** **a** List all the factors of

    **i** 21 _____    **ii** 22 _____

    **iii** 23 _____    **iv** 25_____

  **b** Which number in part **a** is prime?

  _____

**3** List all the prime numbers between 20 and 30.

_____

_____

**4** Here is a list of numbers    84    85    86    87    88    89    90

  Which is the **only** prime number in the list?

_____

**5** Give a reason why each of these numbers is **not** prime.

  **a** 252 _____    **b** 85 _____    **c** 999 _____

**6** Write 35 as the product of two prime numbers.

> Hint: The **product** of 4 and 6 is 24 because $4 \times 6 = 24$.

_____

**7** Write each of the following numbers as the product of two prime numbers.

  **a** 26 = _____    **b** 33 = _____    **c** 65 = _____

**8** Work out these products of prime numbers.

  **a** $2 \times 2 \times 3 =$ _____    **b** $5 \times 2 \times 7 =$ _____

  **c** $2 \times 5 \times 11 =$ _____    **d** $5 \times 5 \times 5 =$ _____

**9** Work out the following calculations.

**a** $5 \times 2 \times 2 =$ _____

**b** $5 \times 2 \times 2 \times 7 =$ _____

**10** 28 written as a product of prime numbers is $2 \times 2 \times 7$.
Write each of each of the following numbers as a product of prime numbers.

**a** $18 =$

**b** $77 =$

_____

_____

**c** $30 =$

**d** $32 =$

_____

_____

# 1.4 Lowest common multiple and highest common factor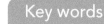

**1**   **a**  Write down the first six multiples of 6.

_____

**b**  Write down the first six multiples of 4.

_____

**c**  Write down two common multiples of 6 and 4.

_____

**d**  Write down the **lowest** common multiple of 6 and 4.

_____

**2**   Find the lowest common multiple of the following:

**a**  2 and 5 _____

**b**  4 and 5 _____

**c**  6 and 5 _____

**d**  10 and 5 _____

**3**   Find the lowest common multiple of 2, 3 and 4.

_____

_____

**4** Find the lowest common multiple of 5, 10 and 25.

_____

_____

**5**　**a** List the factors of 12.

_____

**b** List the factors of 18.

_____

**c** Find the common factors of 12 and 18.

_____

**d** Find the **highest** common factors of 12 and 18.

_____

**6**　**a** Find the common factors of 20 and 30.

_____

**b** Find the highest common factor of 20 and 30.

_____

**7**　**a** Find the highest common factor of 40 and 100.

_____

_____

**b** Write $\frac{40}{100}$ as simply as possible.

_____

**8** Find the highest common factor of 45, 60 and 75.

_____

_____

_____

_____

# 1 Problem solving

**1** 60 chairs are put into rows in a hall. There are the same numbers of chairs in each row. All the chairs are used.

   **a** Show that there could be 10 chairs in each row.

   _____

   _____

   **b** Show that there **cannot** be 8 chairs in each row.

   _____

   _____

   **c** There is not enough space for more than 14 chairs in each row.

     **i** Find the largest possible number of **rows**.

     _____

     _____

     **ii** Find the smallest possible number of rows.

     _____

**2** 10 can be written as the sum of two prime numbers in two different ways:

$$10 = 3 + 7 \quad \text{or} \quad 10 = 5 + 5$$

   **a** Find **two** ways to write 14 as the sum of two prime numbers.

   | Hint: | What are the primes that are less than 14? |

   _____

   **b** Find all the ways to write 24 as the sum of two primes.

   _____

   _____

   **c** Show that 11 is a prime factor of 385.

   | Hint: | Divide 385 by 11. |

   _____

   _____

**d** 385 has two other prime factors. What are they?

Hint: Use your answer to part **c**.

_____

**e** 385 has eight factors altogether. You have found three of them. Find the other five.

_____

_____

_____

**Checklist**

I can

☐ list the multiples of a whole number

☐ list the factors of a number

☐ work out the lowest common multiples of two numbers

☐ work out the highest common factor of two numbers

☐ identify prime numbers.

1 Multiples, factors and primes

# 2 Fractions, decimals and percentages

## 2.1 Equivalent fractions

**Key words**

equivalent fraction

numerator

improper fraction

mixed number

 **1** Write down the fraction shaded. Simplify the fractions as much as possible.

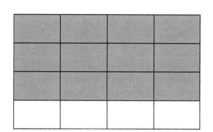

a _____

b _____

c _____

**2** Simplify these fractions as much as possible.

a $\frac{2}{8}$ = _____

b $\frac{4}{10}$ = _____

c $\frac{4}{6}$ = _____

d $\frac{6}{12}$ = _____

**3** Fill in the missing numerators in these equivalent fractions.

a $\frac{1}{2} = \frac{\square}{6}$

b $\frac{3}{5} = \frac{\square}{10}$

c $\frac{1}{2} = \frac{\square}{12}$

d $\frac{6}{8} = \frac{\square}{4}$

e $\frac{3}{2} = \frac{\square}{4}$

f $\frac{2}{3} = \frac{\square}{12}$

g $\frac{3}{4} = \frac{\square}{12}$

h $\frac{5}{2} = \frac{\square}{6}$

**4** Write down three fractions equivalent to $\frac{9}{12}$.

$\frac{9}{12}$ = _____ = _____ = _____

**5** What fraction of £24 are each of the following?

a £12 _____

b £8 _____

c £6 _____

d £18 _____

Write your answers as simply as possible.

**6** Fill in the missing fraction. Write your answer as simply as possible.

a 20 kg is _____ of 30 kg

b 20p is _____ of 32p

c 20 cm is _____ of 50 cm

d 60 years is _____ of 80 years

**7** Add these fractions. Write the answer as simply as possible.

a $\dfrac{1}{2} + \dfrac{1}{2} =$ _____

b $\dfrac{2}{5} + \dfrac{1}{5} =$ _____

c $\dfrac{3}{8} + \dfrac{1}{8} =$ _____

d $\dfrac{3}{10} + \dfrac{1}{10} =$ _____

e $\dfrac{7}{10} + \dfrac{3}{10} =$ _____

f $\dfrac{5}{8} + \dfrac{5}{8} =$ _____

**8** Write these fractions as mixed numbers. The first one has been done for you.

a $\dfrac{7}{4} = 1\dfrac{3}{4}$

b $\dfrac{5}{4} =$ _____

c $\dfrac{9}{4} =$ _____

d $\dfrac{3}{2} =$ _____

e $\dfrac{7}{2} =$ _____

f $\dfrac{11}{8} =$ _____

g $\dfrac{17}{8} =$ _____

h $\dfrac{17}{10} =$ _____

i $\dfrac{33}{10} =$ _____

**9** Write these numbers as improper fractions.

a $5\dfrac{1}{2} =$ _____

b $3\dfrac{1}{4} =$ _____

c $2\dfrac{3}{8} =$ _____

d $5\dfrac{2}{3} =$ _____

**10** Here are four fractions $\qquad \dfrac{1}{2} \qquad \dfrac{2}{3} \qquad \dfrac{2}{5} \qquad \dfrac{3}{4}$

Put them in order, smallest first

_____

## 2.2 Arithmetic with fractions

denominator

**1** a Fill in the missing numerator $\dfrac{3}{4} = \dfrac{\square}{8}$

b Use your answer to part **a** to work out $\dfrac{1}{8} + \dfrac{3}{4} =$ _____

**2** a Fill in the missing numerator $\dfrac{1}{3} = \dfrac{\square}{9}$

b Use your answer to part **a** to work out $\dfrac{1}{3} + \dfrac{2}{9} =$ _____

**3** Fill in the missing numerators in the following additions.

a $\dfrac{1}{4} + \dfrac{1}{2} = \dfrac{1}{4} + \dfrac{\square}{4} = \dfrac{\square}{4}$

b $\dfrac{1}{8} + \dfrac{3}{4} = \dfrac{1}{8} + \dfrac{\square}{8} = \dfrac{\square}{8}$

Hint: To add two fractions, make the denominators (bottom numbers) the same.

c $\dfrac{1}{6} + \dfrac{1}{2} = \dfrac{1}{6} + \dfrac{\square}{6} = \dfrac{\square}{6} = \dfrac{\square}{3}$

d $\dfrac{1}{2} + \dfrac{1}{10} = \dfrac{\square}{10} + \dfrac{1}{10} = \dfrac{\square}{10} = \dfrac{\square}{5}$

**4** Work out the following additions:

a $\frac{1}{4} + \frac{1}{4} =$ _____

b $\frac{1}{8} + \frac{1}{4} =$ _____

c $\frac{3}{8} + \frac{1}{4} =$ _____

d $\frac{5}{8} + \frac{1}{4} =$ _____

e $\frac{1}{10} + \frac{1}{2} =$ _____

f $\frac{1}{2} + \frac{3}{10} =$ _____

**5** Do these subtractions. Write the answers as simply as possible.

a $\frac{2}{3} - \frac{1}{3} =$ _____

b $\frac{4}{5} - \frac{1}{5} =$ _____

c $\frac{7}{10} - \frac{2}{10} =$ _____

d $\frac{9}{10} - \frac{1}{10} =$ _____

e $\frac{7}{8} - \frac{1}{8} =$ _____

f $\frac{5}{8} - \frac{3}{8} =$ _____

**6** Work out these subtractions. Write the answers as simply as possible.

a $\frac{1}{2} - \frac{1}{4} =$ _____

b $\frac{1}{2} - \frac{1}{8} =$ _____

c $\frac{5}{8} - \frac{1}{4} =$ _____

d $\frac{7}{8} - \frac{1}{2} =$ _____

e $\frac{1}{2} - \frac{1}{10} =$ _____

f $\frac{1}{2} - \frac{3}{10} =$ _____

**7** Multiply these fractions by whole numbers. The first one has been done for you.
Write the answers as simply as possible.

a $\frac{2}{3} \times 5 = \frac{10}{3} = 3\frac{1}{3}$

b $\frac{1}{2} \times 7 =$ _____

c $\frac{1}{4} \times 5 =$ _____

d $\frac{3}{4} \times 5 =$ _____

e $\frac{1}{3} \times 6 =$ _____

f $\frac{4}{5} \times 4 =$ _____

**8** Work these out.

a $\frac{1}{3}$ of 7 = _____

b $\frac{2}{3}$ of 4 = _____

c $\frac{3}{4}$ of 6 = _____

Hint: $\frac{1}{3}$ of 7 is the same as $\frac{1}{3} \times 7$

d $\frac{4}{5}$ of 3 = _____

e $\frac{3}{8}$ of 6 = _____

f $\frac{7}{10}$ of 5 = _____

**9** Complete this multiplication table. Write the answers as simply as possible.

| × | $\frac{1}{4}$ | $\frac{1}{3}$ | $\frac{1}{2}$ | $\frac{2}{3}$ | $\frac{3}{4}$ |
|---|---|---|---|---|---|
| 3 |  | 1 |  |  |  |
| 5 |  |  | $2\frac{1}{2}$ |  |  |

# 2.3 Fractions and decimals

**1** Write these fractions as decimals.

**a** $\frac{1}{4}$ = _____   **b** $\frac{3}{4}$ = _____   **c** $2\frac{1}{2}$ = _____   **d** $5\frac{1}{4}$ = _____

**2** Write these fractions as decimals.

**a** $\frac{3}{10}$ = _____   **b** $\frac{9}{10}$ = _____   **c** $\frac{11}{10}$ = _____   **d** $\frac{27}{10}$ = _____

**3** Write these decimals as fractions. Simplify the answers as much as possible.

**a** 0.4 = _____   **b** 0.8 = _____   **c** 0.6 = _____   **d** 1.2 = _____

**4** Write these decimals as fractions. Simplify the answers as much as possible.

**a** 0.15 = _____   **b** 0.35 = _____   **c** 0.45 = _____   **d** 3.55 = _____

**5** Complete this number line by writing the fractions as decimals. The first one has been done for you.

**6** Here is a number line. Write A, B, C and D as decimals and as mixed numbers.

A = _____ = _____         B = _____ = _____

C = _____ = _____         D = _____ = _____

**7** Write these mixed numbers as decimals.

**a** $8\frac{3}{10}$ = _____   **b** $4\frac{1}{4}$ = _____   **c** $6\frac{3}{5}$ = _____   **d** $5\frac{1}{8}$ = _____

**8** Write these decimals as mixed numbers.

**a** 9.7 = _____   **b** 12.8 = _____   **c** 10.75 = _____   **d** 8.125 = _____

**9** Write the answers to these multiplications as mixed numbers **and** as decimals.

**a** $\frac{3}{10} \times 4$ = _____   **b** $\frac{2}{5} \times 4$ = _____

**c** $\frac{3}{4} \times 5$ = _____   **d** $\frac{7}{8} \times 6$ = _____

**10** $\frac{1}{3} = 0.333...$

Write these fractions as decimals in the same way.

**a** $\frac{2}{3} =$ _____  **b** $\frac{1}{9} =$ _____  **c** $\frac{5}{9} =$ _____

**11** Write these numbers in order of size, smallest first.

Hint: First write them as decimals.

$\frac{2}{3}$　　　　$\frac{4}{5}$　　　　$\frac{5}{8}$　　　　$\frac{7}{10}$

smallest _____ largest

# 2.4 Percentages 🔢

**1** 37% of the top bar is purple.

10% of the bottom bar is purple.

| 37% | |
|---|---|

| 10% | |
|---|---|

What percentages of each bar are light blue?

_____

**2** Write these percentages as decimals.

**a** 44% = _____  **b** 40% = _____  **c** 4% = _____

**3** Complete the following table.

| Decimal | 0.5 | 0.35 | 0.77 | 0.6 | | |
|---|---|---|---|---|---|---|
| Percentage | | | | | 80% | 6% |

**4** Complete the following table. Write the fractions as simply as possible.

| Percentage | 25% | 70% | 5% | | | 15% |
|---|---|---|---|---|---|---|
| Fraction | | | | $\frac{3}{4}$ | $\frac{9}{10}$ | |

**5** A group of people are in a room. Two-fifths are adult men and 45% are adult women.

The rest are children.

What percentage are children? _____

**6** This is a sum of percentages. 25% + 20% = 45%

Change the percentages to fractions. _____ + _____ = _____

**7** Work out these percentages of £20.

a 25% _____          b 10% _____          c 70% _____

d 75% _____          e 20% _____          f 80% _____

**8** a Write 20% as a fraction. _____

b Work out 20% of

   i £15 _____          ii £40 _____          iii £2.50 _____

   iv 55 kg _____          v 35 cm _____          vi 80 m_____

**9** Complete the following table.

|       | £10 | £40 | £50 | £80 | £200 |
|-------|-----|-----|-----|-----|------|
| 75%   |     | £30 |     |     |      |
| 40%   |     |     | £20 |     |      |

## 2.5 Working with fractions and percentages

**Key words**

increase

decrease

**1** Work out

a $\frac{1}{4}$ of 40 kg = _____          b $\frac{2}{3}$ of 18 m = _____

c $\frac{3}{4}$ of 60 people = _____          d $\frac{3}{10}$ of 120 kg = _____

e $\frac{5}{6}$ of 30 g = _____          f $\frac{3}{5}$ of 35 m = _____

**2** a What **fraction** of £40 is £8? _____

Hint: Simplify the fraction $\frac{8}{40}$

b What **percentage** of £40 is £8? _____

**3 a** What fraction of 60 people is

    **i** 45 people _____      **ii** 18 people _____      **iii** 36 people _____

    _____        _____        _____

**b** Write your answers to part **a** as percentages.

    **i** _____        **ii** _____        **iii** _____

**4 a** Write 32% as a decimal. _____

**b** Use a calculator to work out 32% of the following.

    **i** £200 _____  **ii** £120 _____  **iii** £25 _____  **iv** £6 _____

**5 a** Write as a decimal

    **i** 8% _____        **ii** 45% _____

**b** Use a calculator to complete this table.

|  | £25 | £40 | £50 | £240 |
|---|---|---|---|---|
| **8%** |  | £3.20 |  |  |
| **45%** | £11.25 |  |  |  |

**6 a** Work out 10% of £60 _____

**b** Increase £60 by 10% _____

**c** Decrease £60 by 10% _____

**7 a** Work out 40% of £80 _____

**b** Increase £80 by 40% _____

**c** Decrease £80 by 40% _____

**8 a** Work out 5% of 120 kg _____

**b** Increase 120 kg by 5% _____

**c** Decrease 120 kg by 5% _____

**9** Jon pays rent of £650 a month. His rent is increased to £676 a month.
Show that this is a 4% increase.

_____

_____

## 2 Problem solving  🖩

**1** **40** people live in Main Street.

18 own a bicycle.

60% take regular exercise.

$\frac{3}{8}$ are under 18 years old.

**a** What fraction take regular exercise? Write the answer as simply as possible.

Hint: Start with the percentage you are given.

_____

**b** How many are under 18? _____

_____

**c** What **percentage** own a bicycle? _____

_____

90 people live in Back Road. 60% own a bicycle.

**d** How many **more** bicycles are there in Back Road than there are Main Street? Show your working.

_____

_____

**2** **a** This is an advert in a shop.

BUY TWO and get the second HALF PRICE

Shower gel £6

**i** How much money do you save if you buy two?

_____

**ii** What is the **percentage** saving if you buy two?

Hint: Write the saving as a percentage of the full price.

_____

**b** Here is an advert about a sale.

**i** The original price of a coat is £80. Find the sale price. Show your working.

_____

_____

**ii** This is the price ticket on a designer handbag.

Is this a 40% reduction? Give a reason for your answer.

_____

_____

**Checklist**

I can

☐ find equivalent fractions

☐ add and subtract fractions

☐ multiply a fraction by a whole number

☐ convert between fractions, decimals and percentages

☐ work out percentages of a quantity

☐ increase or decrease amounts by a percentage.

# 3 Working with numbers

## 3.1 Order of operations

**Key word**
bracket

**1** Work out each of the following.

**a** $3 \times 2 + 5 = $ _____  **b** $4 \times 4 + 4 = $ _____  **c** $4 \times 4 \div 2 = $ _____

**d** $4 \times 4 - 4 = $ _____  **e** $5 + 3 \times 2 = $ _____  **f** $4 + 5 \times 5 = $ _____

**2** Work out each of the following.

Hint: Work the brackets out first.

**a** $2 \times (3 + 3) = $ _____  **b** $10 \div (3 + 2) = $ _____  **c** $(3 + 7) \div 2 = $ _____

**d** $(3 + 7) \times 5 = $ _____  **e** $5 \times (2 + 3) = $ _____  **f** $6 \times (3 - 2) = $ _____

**3** Draw a line from each calculation on the left to the correct answer on the right.

**a** $2 \times 2 + 6$     12     **b** $2 + 6 \div 3$     2

**c** $5 - 1 \times 4$     10     **d** $(3 + 5) \div 4$     5

**e** $4 \times (5 - 2)$     1     **f** $20 \div (7 - 3)$     4

**4** Are the following statements true or false? If true, write T. If false, write F followed by the correct answer.

**a** $12 + 6 \div 3 = 6$ _____  **b** $14 - 4 \times 2 = 20$ _____

**c** $16 \div 2 + 2 = 10$ _____  **d** $8 - 2 \times 2 = 4$ _____

**e** $2 + 4 \times 3 = 14$ _____  **f** $6 \times 2 + 8 = 20$ _____

**g** $21 - 8 \times 2 = 26$ _____  **h** $(12 - 3) \times 4 = 36$ _____

**i** $20 \div (5 + 5) = 9$ _____  **j** $(40 - 20) \div 10 = 38$ _____

**5** James says that $14 - 4 \times 2 = 20$. James is wrong. What was his mistake?

_____

_____

_____

**6** Put in three different numbers to make the following calculation correct.

_____ + _____ × _____ = 17

**7** Work out the following calculations.

**a** $3 \times 3 + 4 \times 4 =$ _____ **b** $(12 - 8) - (5 - 3) =$ _____ **c** $(3 + 7) \times (10 - 4)$

## 3.2 Powers and roots 🖩

| Key words |
|---|
| square |
| square root |
| cube |
| cube root |
| power |

**1** $4^2 = 4 \times 4 = 16$

> **Hint:** Read $4^2$ as 'four squared'.

Write down the following.

**a** $3^2 =$ _____ **b** $7^2 =$ _____ **c** $10^2 =$ _____

**2** Work out the following.

**a** $4^2 + 5^2 =$ _____ **b** $6^2 + 7^2 =$ _____

**3** Work out the following.

**a** $1.3^2 =$ _____ **b** $3.5^2 =$ _____ **c** $4.6^2 =$ _____

**4** $5^2 = 25$, so the **square root** of 25 is 5. We write $\sqrt{25} = 5$.

Write down the following square roots.

**a** $\sqrt{36} =$ _____ **b** $\sqrt{81} =$ _____ **c** $\sqrt{144} =$ _____

**d** $\sqrt{225} =$ _____ **e** $\sqrt{900} =$ _____ **f** $\sqrt{1024} =$ _____

**5** Use a calculator to work out the following.

**a** $\sqrt{1.96} =$ _____ **b** $\sqrt{9.61} =$ _____ **c** $\sqrt{70.56} =$ _____

**6** $4^3 = 4 \times 4 \times 4 = 64$.

> **Hint:** Read this as '4 cubed'.

Work out the following.

**a** $5^3 =$ _____ **b** $2^3 =$ _____ **c** $6^3 =$ _____ **d** $10^3 =$ _____

**7** Work out the following.

**a** $1.1^3 =$ _____ **b** $2.6^3 =$ _____ **c** $8.1^3 =$ _____

**8** $64 = 4 \times 4 \times 4 = 4^3$

> **Hint:** 4 is called the **cube root** of 64. We write $\sqrt[3]{64} = 4$

Find the following cube roots.

**a** $\sqrt[3]{8} =$ _____ **b** $\sqrt[3]{125} =$ _____ **c** $\sqrt[3]{1000} =$ _____ **d** $\sqrt[3]{512} =$ _____

**9** $5^4 = 5 \times 5 \times 5 \times 5 = 625$

> **Hint:** Read this as '5 to the power 4'.

Work out the following.

**a** $2^4 =$ _____ **b** $4^4 =$ _____ **c** $2^6 =$ _____

**10** Which is larger, $3^4$ or $4^3$? Give a reason for your answer.

_____

_____

**11** Write the following in order of size, smallest first: $4^3$, $3^2$, $2^4$

smallest _____ largest

# 3.3 Rounding numbers 🔢

**Key words**

decimal place

significant figure

**1** Write each number to the nearest 10.

**a** 38 _____ **b** 682 _____ **c** 248 _____

**2** Round the following numbers to the nearest 100.

**a** 427 _____ **b** 3580 _____ **c** 3087 _____

**3** Round the following numbers to the nearest 1000.

**a** 4179 _____ **b** 5821 _____ **c** 18 706 _____

**4** Write each number to the nearest whole number.

a 42.7 _____ b 51.9 _____ c 2.4 _____

d 3.5 _____ e 11.8 _____ f 15.1 _____

g 3.23 _____ h 81.22 _____ i 98.61 _____

j 66.53 _____ k 13.45 _____ l 8.99 _____

**5** Circle the value of each number to 1 decimal place. The first one has been done for you.

a 5.24 (5.2) or 5.3    b 6.75    6.7    or    6.8

c 8.88    8.8    or    8.9    d 14.53    14.5    or    14.6

e 11.621    11.6    or    11.7    f 58.452    58.4    or    58.5

g 8.554    8.5    or    8.6    h 3.751    3.7    or    3.8

**6** Work out the following square roots. Write your answers to 1 decimal place.

a $\sqrt{75}$ = _____ b $\sqrt{130}$ = _____ c $\sqrt{201}$ = _____

**7** Write each of the following to 2 decimal places.

a 4.6666 _____ b 3.34343 _____ c 8.8755 _____

d $\sqrt{5}$ _____ e $\sqrt{52}$ _____ f $\sqrt{90}$ _____

**8** Change the following fractions to decimals. Round your answer to 2 decimal places.

a $\frac{2}{3}$ = _____ b $\frac{1}{6}$ = _____ c $\frac{5}{6}$ = _____

Hint: $\frac{2}{3} = 2 \div 3$

**9** Round the following numbers to 1 significant figure.

Hint: Only one digit in the answer is not 0.

a 821 _____ b 394 _____ c 6129 _____

d 7293 _____ e 4830 _____ f 58631 _____

# 3.4 Standard form ✕

**1** Write the following as ordinary numbers.

    **a** $10^2 =$ _____    **b** $10^3 =$ _____    **c** $10^5 =$ _____

**2** Write the following as powers of ten.

    **a** one thousand _____    **b** ten thousand _____    **c** one million _____

**3** Work out the following.

    **a** $15 \times 10 =$ _____    **b** $24 \times 100 =$ _____    **c** $38 \times 1000 =$ _____

**4** Work out the following.

    **a** $7.3 \times 10 =$ _____    **b** $5.8 \times 100 =$ _____    **c** $2.9 \times 1000 =$ _____

**5** Fill in the following missing numbers.    Hint: It will be 10 or 100 or 1000.

    **a** $3 \times$ _____ $= 300$   **b** $4.9 \times$ _____ $= 490$   **c** $4.25 \times$ _____ $= 4250$

**6** In **standard form** $6500 = 6.5 \times 10^3$

    Hint: Standard form is a number between 1 and 10 times a power of 10.

    Write the following numbers in standard form.

    **a** $3200 =$ _____    **b** $6000 =$ _____    **c** $1230 =$ _____

**7** Write the following numbers in standard form.

    **a** $40\,000 =$ _____    **b** $73\,000 =$ _____    **c** $260\,000 =$ _____

    **d** $803\,000 =$ _____    **e** $7\,000\,000 =$ _____    **f** $4\,800\,000 =$ _____

**8** The following numbers are in standard form. Write them as ordinary numbers.

    **a** $9 \times 10^2 =$ _____    **b** $9.2 \times 10^2 =$ _____    **c** $3 \times 10^5 =$ _____

    **d** $1.8 \times 10^6 =$ _____    **e** $4.75 \times 10^5 =$ _____    **f** $1.41 \times 10^4 =$ _____

**9**   $A = 9.3 \times 10^4$       $B = 4.8 \times 10^3$       $C = 3.57 \times 10^4$       $D = 1.101 \times 10^5$

    Write A, B, C and D in order of size, smallest first.   Hint: Write them as ordinary numbers.

_____

    smallest _____ largest

**10** Do the following additions. Give your answers in standard form.

**a** $2 \times 10^5 + 3.1 \times 10^5 =$ _____

**b** $2 \times 10^4 + 3.1 \times 10^5 =$ _____

# 3.5 Units 🏁

**Key words**

litre

24-hour clock

**1** In the 24-hour clock, 9:30 am is 09:30 and 9:45 pm is 21:45.
How many minutes are there between these times?

**a** 15:15 and 15:40 _____    **b** 07:45 and 08:30 _____

**c** 09:10 and 10:10 _____    **d** 13:40 and 14:30 _____

**2** Circle the possible height of a woman

0.165 m          1.65 m          16.5 m          165 m

**3** Circle the possible mass of a man

0.74 kg          7.4 kg          74 kg          740 kg

**4** Circle the most likely time for an adult to walk 4.5 km.

45 seconds          4.5 minutes          45 minutes          4.5 hours

**5** Fill in the missing numbers.

Hint: 1 litre = 1000 ml.

**a** 2 litres = _____ ml   **b** $1\frac{1}{2}$ litres = _____ ml   **c** $\frac{1}{4}$ litre = _____ ml

**6** Write down a sensible **metric** unit to measure the following.

**a** The length of your foot _____    **b** The capacity of a glass _____

**c** The mass of a baby _____    **d** The distance between two towns _____

**e** The mass of a spoonful of sugar_____    **f** The length of a room _____

**7** Fill in the missing numbers.

**a** 90 mm = _____ cm          **b** 4 m = _____ cm

**c** 2 km = _____ m          **d** half a metre = _____ cm

**e** half a kilometre = _____ m          **f** 5.3 cm = _____ mm

**8** Write the following lengths in metres.

**a** 3.5 km = _____ m   **b** 4.65 km = _____ m   **c** 0.35 km = _____ m

**9** Write the following quantities in ml.

**a** 6.5 litres = _____ ml  **b** 2.85 litres = _____ ml  **c** 0.61 litres = _____ ml

**10** **a** A film starts at 16:40 and lasts 100 minutes. At what time does it finish?

_____

**b** A train journey starts at 09:55 and take 4 hours and 10 minutes. At what time does it end?

_____

## 3 Problem solving

**1** Here are four number cards.

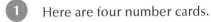

**a** Using two of the cards, fill in the missing numbers to make the following calculation correct.

2 × _____ + 3 × _____ = 22

**b** Using each card once, fill in the missing numbers to make the following calculation correct.

_____ × _____ + _____ × _____ = 23

**c** Using each card once, make the largest possible answer using the following calculation.

_____ × _____ + _____ × _____ = _____

**d** This is a different calculation. Use each card once to make the largest possible answer.

(_____ + _____) × (_____ + _____) = _____

**2**   Here are the populations of three towns.

| Town | Grimsby | Blackpool | Sunderland |
|---|---|---|---|
| Population | 88 251 | 126 398 | 287 705 |

**a** Round each population to the nearest thousand. The first one has been done for you.

| Town | Grimsby | Blackpool | Sunderland |
|---|---|---|---|
| Population | 88 000 | | |

**b** Round the population of each town to 1 significant figure.

| Town | Grimsby | Blackpool | Derby |
|---|---|---|---|
| Population | | | |

**c** Find the total population of the three towns. Round your answer to the nearest thousand. Write your answer in standard form.

_____

_____

**Checklist**

I can

☐ carry out operations in the correct order

☐ work out squares, cubes, square roots, cube roots and powers

☐ round numbers to the nearest thousand, to the nearest whole number, to a number of decimal places or to 1 significant figure

☐ understand and use numbers in standard form

☐ convert metric units.

# 4 Sequences of numbers

## 4.1 Describing a sequence 🔲

**1** Write down the next number in each sequence.

**a** 8, 10, 12, 14, _____   **b** 7, 10, 13, 16, _____

**c** 10, 14, 18, 22, _____   **d** 21, 19, 17, 15, _____

**e** 31, 36, 41, 46, _____   **f** 56, 52, 48, 44, _____

| Key words |
| --- |
| sequence |
| term |
| term-to-term rule |

**2**  **a** Write the next four numbers in the sequence.

13, 16, 19, 22, _____, _____, _____, _____

**b** State the rule that you used.

_____

**3** Fill in the missing numbers.

**a** 15, 19, 23, _____, 31, 35   **b** 44, 48, _____, 56, 60

**c** 70, 67, _____, 61, 58   **d** 22, _____, 30, 34, 38

**e** 50, _____, 62, 68, 74   **f** 42, 33, _____, 15, 6

**4** Look at this sequence   5, 8, 11, 14, 17, 20, 23, …   Hint:  5 + 3 = 8; 8 + 3 = 11; 11 + 3 = 14
The **term-to-term rule** is **add 3**.
Write down the term-to-term rule for each sequence.

**a** 20, 25, 30, 35, … _____   **b** 10, 17, 24, 31, … _____

**c** 24, 22, 20, 18, … _____   **d** 25, 21, 17, 13, … _____

**5** The first term is 8. The term-to-term rule is **add 5**.

**a** Write down the next two terms _____

**b** Work out the 6th term _____

**6** 2, 4, 8, 16, 32, ….

The term-to term rule is **multiply** by 2.

Write down the term-to-term rule for each sequence.

**a** 3, 6, 12, 24, 48, … _____

**b** 2, 6, 18, 54, 162, … _____

**c** 2, 10, 50, 250, 1250, 6250… _____

**d** 1, 4, 16, 64, 256, … _____

**7** The first term is 5. The term-to-term rule is multiply by 2. Write down the next three terms.

_____

**8** 100, 88, 76, 64, …

**a** Next term = _____

**b** Term-to-term rule = _____

# 4.2 Recognising sequences

**1**

$1^2 = 1 \times 1 = 1$     $2^2 = 2 \times 2 = 4$     $3^2 = 3 \times 3 = 9$

1, 4 and 9 are the first three **square numbers**.

**a** Write down the next three square numbers.

$4^2 =$ _____ $5^2 =$ _____ $6^2 =$ _____

**b** Write down these square numbers.

$8^2 =$ _____ $10^2 =$ _____

**Key words**

square numbers

cube numbers

triangle numbers

**2** Circle the square numbers

25      35      49      60      81      110      121

**3** **a** Write down the differences between the square numbers.

> Hint:  $4 - 1 = 3$; $9 - 4 = ...$

1          4          9          16          25          36

     3        _____      _____      _____      _____

**b** What do you notice about your answers?

_____

**4** $1^3 = 1 \times 1 \times 1 = 1$      $2^3 = 2 \times 2 \times 2 = 8$      $3^3 = 3 \times 3 \times 3 = 27$

These are the first three **cube** numbers. Write down the next three.

$4^3 =$ _____      $5^3 =$ _____      $6^3 =$ _____

**5** Show that 1000 is a cube number.

_____

**6**

1     1 + 2 = 3     1 + 2 + 3 = 6

These are the first three **triangle numbers**.

**a** Show that the 4th triangle number is 10.

_____

**b** 5th triangle number = _____

**c** 6th triangle number = _____

**d** 10th triangle number = _____

**7** Show that 64 is both a square number and a cube number.

_____

## 4.3 The $n$th term of a sequence 🖩

**Key word**

$n$th term

**1** If $n = 4$ work out the following.

    **a** $n + 1 =$ _____    **b** $n + 5 =$ _____    **c** $n - 3 =$ _____    **d** $n + 10 =$ _____

**2** If $n = 3$ work out the following.

    **a** $2n =$ _____    **b** $4n =$ _____    **c** $5n =$ _____    **d** $10n =$ _____

**3** If $n = 4$ work out the following.

    **a** $2n =$ _____    **b** $2n + 5 =$ _____    **c** $2n - 5 =$ _____    **d** $2(n + 1) =$ _____

**4** Complete the following table.

| $n$ | 1 | 2 | 3 | 4 | 5 |
|---|---|---|---|---|---|
| $2n + 4$ | | 8 | | | |

**5** Complete the following table.

| n | 1 | 2 | 3 | 4 | 5 |
|---|---|---|---|---|---|
| **2(n + 1)** | | 6 | | | |

**6** Work out $3n - 2$ when

**a** $n = 1$ _____ **b** $n = 4$ _____ **c** $n = 5$ _____ **d** $n = 10$ _____

**7** The nth term of a sequence is $2n + 5$. Write down the following terms.

Hint: 1st term = $2 \times 1 + 5$

1st = _____ 2nd = _____ 3rd = _____ 4th = _____

**8** The nth term of a sequence is $3n - 2$. Write down the following terms.

1st = _____ 2nd = _____ 3rd = _____ 4th = _____

**9** Draw a line to join each nth term to its sequence.

$2n - 1$          2, 4, 6, 8, 10, …

$2n$          1, 3, 5, 7, 9, …

$2n + 1$          4, 6, 8, 10, 12, …

$2(n + 1)$          3, 5, 7, 9, 11, …

**10** The nth term is $3n + 5$. Work out the following terms.

**a** 2nd term = _____ **b** 6th term = _____ **c** 10th term = _____

**11** The nth term is $10n + 1$.

**a** Write down the first 5 terms

_____

**b** Write down the 10th term

_____

# 4 Problem solving

**Key word**

pattern

**1**  **a** Write down the first five odd numbers.

_____

**b** Add the following odd numbers.

**i** 1st + 2nd = _____  **ii** 2nd + 3rd = _____  **iii** 3rd + 4th = _____  **iv** 4th + 5th = _____

**c** Describe the answers to part **b**.

_____

**d** Write down the first five triangle numbers.

> Hint: Remember they are 1, 1 + 2, …

_____

**e** Add the following triangle numbers.

**i** 1st + 2nd = _____  **ii** 2nd + 3rd = _____  **iii** 3rd + 4th = _____  **iv** 4th + 5th = _____

**f** What type of numbers are the answers to part **b**?

_____

**g** Add the following triangle numbers.

**i** 5th + 6th = _____     **ii** 9th + 10th = _____

**2**  These patterns are made from **dots** and **lines**.

1          2          3          4

Pattern 2 has 6 dots.

**a** Complete the following table.

| Pattern | 1 | 2 | 3 | 4 |
|---------|---|---|---|---|
| Dots    |   | 6 |   |   |

**b** Work out the number of dots in pattern 6.

_____

Pattern 2 has 7 lines.

c Complete the following table.

| Pattern | 1 | 2 | 3 | 4 |
|---------|---|---|---|---|
| Lines | | 7 | | |

d Work out the number of lines in pattern 7.

_____

The number of lines in pattern $n$ is $3n + 1$.

e Show this formula is correct for pattern 4.

_____

f Work out the number of lines for pattern 20.

_____

**Checklist**

I can

☐ work out and use the term-to-term rule for a sequence

☐ identify square numbers, cube numbers and triangle numbers

☐ use the $n$th term of a sequence to write down terms.

# 5 Coordinates and graphs

## 5.1 Coordinates

**Key words**

coordinates

midpoint

axis

vertices

vertex

**1**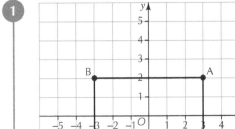

The coordinates of B are (−3, 2).

**a** Write down the coordinates of the other three vertices, A, C and D.

A = _____        C = _____

D = _____

**b** The midpoint of AB is (0, 2). Mark it with a cross.

> **Hint:** Half way between A and B

**c** Put a cross on the midpoint of each of the other sides. Write down their coordinates.

---

**2**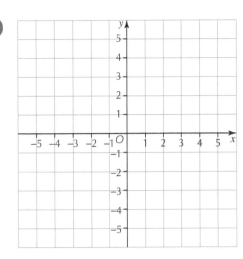

**a** Put these points on the grid. Join them in order with straight lines.

(5, 1)  (5, 3)  (1, 5)  (−3, 3)  (−3, 1)  (1, −1)  (5, 1)

**b** You have drawn a hexagon. Draw the diagonals by joining opposite corners.

**c** Write down the coordinates of the point where the diagonals meet.

_____

**3**

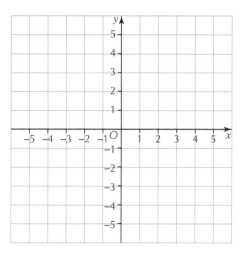

a  Mark each point with a cross. (3, 0) (−1, 2) (5, −1) (−3, 3)

b  Join the points with a straight line.

c  Write down the coordinates of the point where the line crosses the y axis. _____

**4**

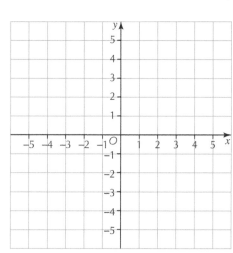

a  Mark **five** points with an x-coordinate of 2.

b  Join them with a straight line.

c  Mark five points with an y-coordinate of −4.

d  Join them with a straight line.

e  Write the coordinates of the point where they cross.

_____

## 5.2 The equation of a straight line

Key word

equation

**1**

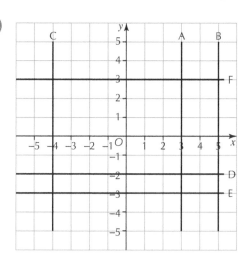

a  The equation of line A is x = 3.
   Write down the equation of
   Line B _____ line C _____

b  The equation of line D is y = −2.
   Write down the equation of

   line E _____

   line F. _____

**2**  **a** Work out the following.

  **i**  $-1 + 3 =$ _____  **ii**  $-2 + 3 =$ _____  **iii**  $-5 + 3 =$ _____

  **b** Complete the following table.

| $x$ | 2 | 0 | –2 | –4 |
|---|---|---|---|---|
| $y = x + 3$ | 5 | | | |

  **c**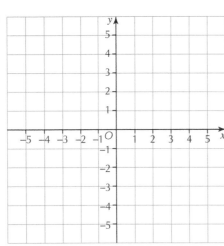

The table gives the coordinates of four points. Plot them on the grid.

  **d** Join the points to show the straight line $y = x + 3$.

  **e** Write down the coordinates of two more points on the line $y = x + 3$.

  _____

**3**  **a** Work out the following.

  **i**  $2 \times -2 =$ _____  **ii**  $2 \times -3 =$ _____  **iii**  $2 \times -5 =$ _____

  **b** Complete the following table.

| $x$ | –2 | –1 | 0 | 1 | 2 |
|---|---|---|---|---|---|
| $y = 2x$ | | –2 | | | |

  **c**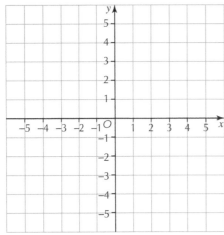

The table gives the coordinates of five points. Plot them on the grid.

  **d** Join the points to show the straight line $y = 2x$.

  **e** Write down the coordinates of one more point on the line $y = 2x$.

  _____

**4**   $x + y = 4$

**a  i**   when $x = 1$, $y =$ _____     **ii**   when $x = 3$, $y =$ _____

**iii**   when $x = 0$, $y =$ _____     **iv**   when $x = 5$, $y =$ _____

**b**  Complete the following table when $x + y = 4$.

| $x$ | −1 | 0 | 1 | 2 | 3 | 4 | 5 |
|---|---|---|---|---|---|---|---|
| $y$ |  |  | 3 |  |  | 0 |  |

**c**  Plot the points on a grid. Join them with a straight line.

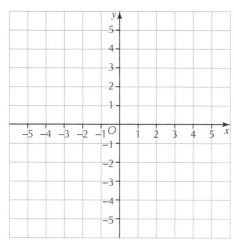

# 5.3 Intercept and gradient

**Key words**

intercept

gradient

**1**   Three points on a straight line are (2, 4), (4, 6) and (−3, −1).

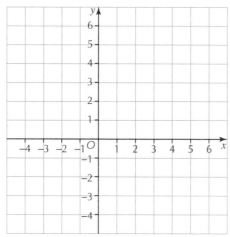

**a**  Draw the line on the grid.

**b**  The **intercepts** are the points where the line crosses the axes.

Write down their coordinates.

_____

**2** The intercepts of a straight line are (6, 0) and (0, 3). Draw the line on the grid.

**a**

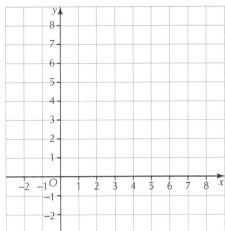

**b** Circle the coordinates of points that are on the line.

(1, 4)    (4, 1)    (8, −1)    (−1, 8)    (3, 2)

**3** Circle the correct answer.

**a** The gradient of line 1 is    1    2    4    8

**b** The gradient of line 2 is    $\frac{1}{9}$    $\frac{1}{3}$    3    9

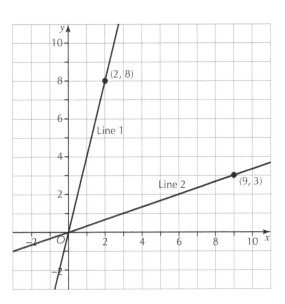

**4** Work out the gradient of the following lines.

**a** OA _____

**b** OB _____

**c** OC _____

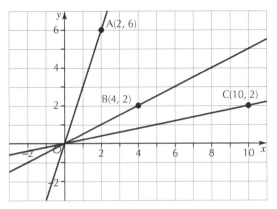

**5** The equation of a straight line is $y = 2x + 4$.

**a** Complete the following table.

| x | −2 | −1 | 0 | 1 | 2 | 3 |
|---|---|---|---|---|---|---|
| $y = 2x + 4$ | 0 | 2 | | | | |

**b** Draw the line on the following grid.

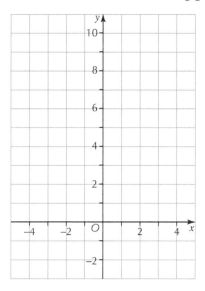

**c** Write down

   **i** the intercept on the y-axis = _____

   **ii** the gradient. _____

## 5.4 Quadratic graphs

**Key word**

quadratic

**1** **a** Complete the following table.

Hint: $4^2$ is $4 \times 4$

| x | 0 | 1 | 2 | 3 | 4 | 5 |
|---|---|---|---|---|---|---|
| $y = x^2$ | 0 | 1 | | | 16 | |

**b** Plot the points on this grid.

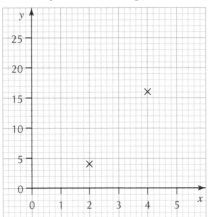

Hint: The scales on the axes are different.

**c** Join the points to draw the graph $y = x^2$.

Hint: Join the points with a smooth curve.

**2** **a** Complete the following table.

| $x$ | 0 | 1 | 2 | 3 | 4 |
|-----|---|---|---|---|---|
| $y = x^2 + 4$ | 4 | | 8 | | |

**b** Plot the points on the following grid.

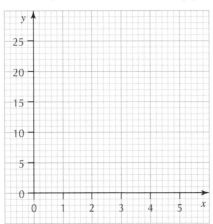

**c** Join the points to draw the graph $y = x^2 + 4$.

**3** **a** Complete the following table.

| $x$ | 0 | 1 | 2 | 3 | 4 | 5 |
|-----|---|---|---|---|---|---|
| $y = x^2 - 10$ | −10 | | −6 | | | |

**b** Draw the graph $y = x^2 - 10$.

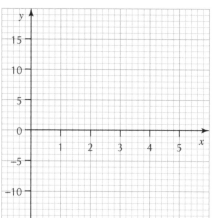

**4**

**a** Work out the following.

Hint: The square of a negative number is positive.

**i** $(-2)^2 =$ _____

**ii** $(-4)^2 =$ _____

**b** Complete the following table.

| $x$ | −4 | −3 | −2 | −1 | 0 | 1 | 2 | 3 | 4 |
|---|---|---|---|---|---|---|---|---|---|
| $y = x^2$ | | | | | | | | | |

**c** Draw the graph $y = x^2$ on this grid.

Hint: The $y$-axis is a line of symmetry.

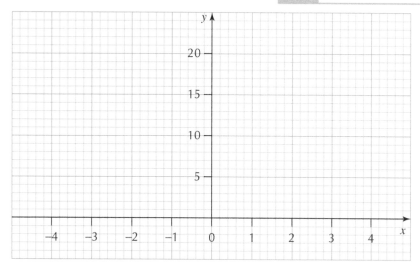

# 5 Problem solving

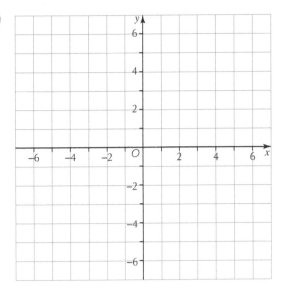

**a** Plot A(6, 3), B(−4, 3) and C(6, −3).

**b** Write down the coordinates of the midpoint of AB. _____

Hint: Draw AB.

**c** Write down the coordinates of the midpoint of AC. _____

**d** Work out the equation of the straight line through A and B. _____

**e** Draw the line $y = x$

**f** Write down the coordinates of the point where AB and $y = x$ cross. _____

**g** A, B and C are three vertices of a rectangle.

Write down the coordinates of the fourth vertex. _____

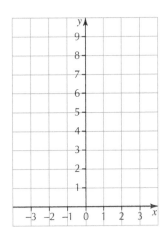

**a** Complete the following table.

| $x$ | 0 | 1 | 2 | 3 |
|---|---|---|---|---|
| $3x$ | | | 6 | |

**b** Draw the line $y = 3x$

**c** Write down the gradient of the line $y = 3x$. _____

**d** Complete the following table.

| $x$ | −3 | −2 | −1 | 0 | 1 | 2 | 3 |
|---|---|---|---|---|---|---|---|
| $x + 6$ | 3 | | | | | 8 | |

**e** Draw the line $y = x + 6$.

**f** Write down the gradient of the line $y = x + 6$. _____

**g** Write down the intercept on the $y$-axis of $y = x + 6$. _____

**h** Complete the following table.

| $x$ | −3 | −2 | −1 | 0 | 1 | 2 | 3 |
|---|---|---|---|---|---|---|---|
| $x^2$ | | 4 | | | | 4 | |

**i** Draw the curve $y = x^2$

**j** Write down the coordinates of the point where the three lines meet. _____

**Checklist**

I can

☐ plot points with positive or negative coordinates

☐ draw a straight line from its equation

☐ find the gradient of a straight line

☐ find the intercepts of a straight line, i.e. where it crosses the axes

☐ draw a simple quadratic curve.

# 6 Expressions and equations

## 6.1 Substituting into formulae &#9187;

**Key words**

expression

formula

substitute

**1** Rex is $R$ years old.

Write an expression using $R$ to write these ages. The first one is done for you.

**a** Keri is 5 years younger than Rex. $R - 5$

**b** Lucy is 4 years older than Rex. _____

**c** Tom is twice the age of Rex. _____

**d** Jose is half the age of Rex. _____

**2** If $w = 6$, what is the value of these expressions?

**a** $w + 9 =$ _____

**b** $w - 5 =$ _____

**c** $w \div 2 =$ _____

**d** $w - 8 =$ _____

**e** $2w =$ _____

**f** $5w =$ _____

**3** $p = 4$ and $q = 6$. Find the values of the following expressions. The first one is done for you.

**a** $5p + 2q = 20 + 12 = 32$

**b** $5p - 2q =$ _____ = _____

**c** $10p + 3q =$ _____ = _____

**d** $\frac{1}{2}p + \frac{1}{2}q =$ _____ = _____

**e** $2(p + q) =$ _____ = _____

**f** $5(q - p) =$ _____ = _____

**4** A formula for estimating the perimeter of a circular pond is

perimeter = 3 × diameter

**a** Work out an estimate of the perimeter of a pond with diameter 4 m.

_____

**b** Work out an estimate of the perimeter of a pond with diameter 6 m.

_____

**5** The formula for the perimeter of a triangle with sides of length $a$, $b$, and $c$ is

$P = a + b + c$

**a** What is the perimeter of the triangle when $a = 3$ cm, $b = 4$ cm and $c = 5$ cm?

_____

**b** What is the perimeter of the triangle when $a = 12$ m, $b = 6$ m and $c = 9$ m?

_____

**6** The cost £C of hiring a car for D days is given by the formula

$C = 20D + 10$

Work out the cost for

**a** 2 days _____

**b** 4 days _____.

**7**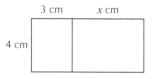

The area of this rectangle is $4(x + 3)$ cm².

Work out the area when

**a** $x = 2$ cm _____

**b** $x = 17$ cm _____.

# 6.2 Simplifying expressions

**1** Simplify as much as possible.

**a** $x + 4x =$ _____

**b** $3y - y =$ _____

**c** $p + 2p + 5p =$ _____

**d** $10t - 3t - 2t =$ _____

**2** Simplify the following expressions as much as possible.

**a** $t + 1 + t + 2 =$ _____

**b** $2x + 1 + 2x - 1 =$ _____

**c** $4 + 4k - 2 - k =$ _____

**d** $n + 1 + 3n - 4 =$ _____

**3**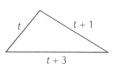

Write an expression for the perimeter of this triangle as simply as possible.

_____

**4** Multiply out the following brackets.

**a** $2(x + 1) =$ _____

**b** $3(y - 2) =$ _____

**c** $4(a + 3) =$ _____

**d** $5(2a - 1) =$ _____

**5** Multiply out the following brackets.

**a** $4(x + y) =$ _____

**b** $3(a + 2b) =$ _____

**6** Draw a line between the following equivalent expressions. One has been done for you.

| | |
|---|---|
| $4(x + 2)$ | $8x + 2$ |
| $2(x + 4)$ | $8x + 4$ |
| $8(x + 1)$ ———————— | $8x + 8$ |
| $2(4x + 1)$ | $2x + 8$ |
| $4(2x + 1)$ | $4x + 8$ |

**7** Factorise the following expressions.

**a** $2c + 10 =$ _____

**b** $3x - 9 =$ _____

**c** $4w + 10 =$ _____

**d** $8n - 2 =$ _____

**8** Factorise the following expressions fully.

**a** $4a + 4b =$ _____

**b** $6x - 12y =$ _____

**c** $20s + 30t =$ _____

**d** $4a + 8b - 12c =$ _____

# 6.3 Solving equations

**1** Solve the following equations.

> **Hint:** Find the answers by subtraction.

**a** $x + 5 = 20$      $x =$ _____

**b** $y + 12 = 19$      $y =$ _____

**2** Solve the following equations.

**a** $2t = 8$      $t =$ _____

**b** $4y = 24$      $y =$ _____

**3** Solve the following equations.

> **Hint:** The answer to part **a** is **not** 3.

**a** $g - 4 = 7$      $g =$ _____

**b** $r - 2 = 10$      $r =$ _____

**4** Solve the following equations.

> **Hint:** Find each answer by doing a multiplication.

**a** $\frac{1}{2}p = 3$      $p =$ _____

**b** $\frac{T}{2} = 9$      $T =$ _____

**5** Solve the following equations.

**a** $2(x + 3) = 14$

**b** $3(y - 2) = 18$

**6** Solve the following equations.

**a** $3y + 5 = 17$

**b** $4x - 3 = 29$

**c** $5w + 12 = 47$

**d** $12g - 32 = 16$

**e** $\dfrac{m}{3} - 8 = 2$

# 6 Problem solving ⚔

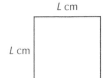

1. This is a square. Each side has length $L$ cm.

   **a** Show that the perimeter of the square is $4L$ cm.

   _____

   **b** Here are two squares put together.

   Write an expression for the perimeter in centimetres.
   Write your answer as simply as possible.

   _____

   **c** This is a rectangle. The sides are $L$ cm and 3 cm.

   This shape is made from two squares
   (in part **a**) and two rectangles.

   Write an expression for the perimeter. Write your answer as simply as possible.

   _____

2. **a**

   ⟩ $x = 1$ ⟩ → ⟩ $x + 5 = 6$ ⟩ → ⟩ $2(x + 5) =$ ⟩

   Write the missing number in the last box.

   **b**

   ⟩ $x = 4$ ⟩ → ⟩ $x + 5 =$ ⟩ → ⟩ $2(x + 5) =$ ⟩

   Write in the two missing numbers.

   **c**

   ⟩ $x =$ ⟩ → ⟩ $x + 5 = 12$ ⟩ → ⟩ $2(x + 5) =$ ⟩

   Write in the two missing numbers.

   **d**

   ⟩ $x =$ ⟩ → ⟩ $x + 5 =$ ⟩ → ⟩ $2(x + 5) = 40$ ⟩

   Write in the two missing numbers.

---

**Checklist**

I can

☐ substitute numbers into formulae

☐ simplify expressions

☐ solve simple equations.

# 7 Ratio and proportion

## 7.1 Ratio notation

**Key word**

ratio

**1** In a class the ratio of boys to girls is 2 : 1. There are 8 girls.
Work out the number of boys.

_____

**2** A hockey team has seven women and four men.

**a** Write down the ratio of women to men.

_____

**b** Write down the ratio of men to women.

_____

**3** A class has 20 girls and 10 boys. Write down the ratio of girls to boys.
Give your ratio as simply as possible.

_____

**4** There are 12 cats and 4 dogs. Complete these sentences.

**a** There are _____ cats for every dog.

**b** The ratio of cats to dogs is _____ : 1

**5** Write these ratios as simply as possible. The first one has been
done for you.

**a** $8 : 4 = 2 : 1$        Hint:   Divide both numbers by 4.

**b** $9 : 3 =$ _____        **c** $20 : 5 =$ _____

**d** $6 : 8 =$ _____        **e** $18 : 12 =$ _____

**f** $10 : 25 =$ _____        **g** $16 : 24 =$ _____

**6** Write down the ratio of red circles to blue circles in the following patterns. Write the ratio as simply as possible.

**a**

_____

**b**

_____

**c**

_____

**7** Here are the ingredients for a recipe.

Write the ratio of the masses of each of the following. Give your answers in simplest form.

**a** tomatoes : cheese = _____

**b** pasta : cheese = _____

> **Recipe**
> Pasta        400 g
> Tomatoes   500 g
> Cheese      250 g

**8** Write down the following ratios for one person as simply as possible.

**a** Noses to toes. _____

**b** Fingers to thumbs. _____

**9** The ratio of cows to sheep in a field is 3 : 2.
Write whether these statements are **true** or **false**.

**a** There are more cows than sheep. _____

**b** Over half the animals are sheep. _____

**c** The ratio of legs to animals is 4 : 1. _____

**d** 3 animals out of 5 are cows. _____

**10** In a group of people one quarter are men and the rest are women.
Work out the ratio of women to men.

_____

**11** $\frac{3}{5}$ of the plates in a cupboard are large. The rest are small.
Work out the ratio of large plates to small plates.

_____

# 7.2 Dividing using a ratio ✗

**Key words**

ratio

fraction

**1** There are 15 children in a room.

One-third are boys and the rest are girls. Work out

**a** the number of boys

_____

**b** the number of girls

_____

**c** the ratio of boys to girls. Write your ratio in its simplest from.

_____

**2** There are 40 vehicles in a car park.

$\frac{3}{4}$ are cars and the rest are vans.

Work out

**a** the number of cars _____

**b** the ratio of cars to vans. Write your ratio in its simplest from.

_____

**3** The ratio of dry days to wet days in June is 5 : 1.

There are 30 days in June.

Work out the number of

**a** wet days _____  **b** dry days. _____

**4** The ratio of apples to oranges in a bowl is 1 : 3.

Work out

**a** the number of oranges if there are 4 apples

_____

**b** the number of apples if there are 18 oranges.

_____

**5** 60 people take a driving test. 10 people fail. The rest pass.

Work out the ratio pass : fail. Write your ratio in its simplest form.

_____

**6** The ratio of girls to boys is 2 : 3.

  **a** If there are 20 children in total, work out the number of girls.

  _____

  **b** If there are 20 girls, work out the number of boys.

  _____

**7** In a recipe the ratio of the mass of flour to the mass of butter is 4 : 1.

  **a** If the total mass is 250 g, work out the mass of butter.

  _____

  **b** If the mass of flour is 80 g, work out the mass of butter.

  _____

# 7.3 Proportion

**1** Sam walks 6 km in 1 hour.
Assume that she walks at a constant speed.
Work out

  **a** the distance that she walks in 3 hours

  _____

  **b** the time that she takes to walk 30 km.

  _____

**2** Ali has 3.5 hours of maths lessons each week.
Work out the number of hours of maths lessons he has in

  **a** 12 weeks _____

  **b** 38 weeks. _____

**3** Karl has a job with an hourly rate of pay.
His pay is £75.20 for 8 hours.
Work out his pay for

  **a** 1 hour _____        **b** 35 hours. _____

  _____                       _____

**4** One litre of petrol costs £1.25.

Work out

a the cost of 23 litres _____

b the number of litres you can buy for £50. _____

**5** Work out

a the flour you need for 1 scone

_____

b the butter you need for 30 scones

_____

c the milk you need for 10 scones.

_____

> *Recipe*
>
> Ingredients for 15 scones
>
> Flour     240 g
>
> Butter    45 g
>
> Milk      150 ml

**6** The scale of the plan of a house is 1 : 20.

On the plan the length of a room is 32 cm.

Work out the actual length of the room

a in centimetres _____     b in metres. _____

**7** 8 km = 5 miles

Work out these missing numbers.

a 20 miles = _____ km     b 20 km = _____ miles

**8** This is a sales ticket in an airport shop.

a Work out how many dollars £1 is worth.

_____

b The price of a handbag is £95.

Work out the price in dollars.

_____

> Scarf £25
> or
> $32.50

**9** €1 = £0.90   Work out the missing numbers.

a €70 = £ _____     b £135 = € _____

= £ _____     = € _____

# 7.4 Ratios and fractions

**1** In a weather survey, the ratio of sunny days to cloudy days is 3 : 1.

    **a** There were five cloudy days. Work out the number of sunny days.

    _____

    **b** Write down the total number of days.

    _____

    **c** Work out the fraction of days that are sunny. Write your answer as simply as possible.

    _____

**2** Bricks in a wall can be headers ▮ or ▭ stretchers.

    Here is a row of bricks.

    **a** Write down the ratio of headers to stretchers.

    _____

    **b** Write down the **fraction** of the bricks that are headers.

    _____

**3** The ratio of tulips to daffodils in a vase of flowers is 1 : 3.

    There are 32 flowers altogether.

    **a** Work out the number of each kind.

    Tulips _____        Daffodils _____

    **b** Work out the fraction of these flowers that are tulips.

    _____

**4** A box contains only red pens and blue pens. The ratio of the number of red pens to the number of blue pens is 2 : 3.

    Write down the fraction of pencils that are red.

    _____

**5** A box contains long and short pencils.

    $\frac{3}{5}$ of the pencils are long.

    Write down the ratio of long pencils : short pencils.

    _____

**6** There are 20 chickens and 25 ducks.

**a** Work out the ratio of chickens to ducks. Write the answer as simply as possible.

_____

**b** Work out the fraction of the birds that are ducks.

_____

**7** Lucy is 120 cm tall. Sam is 40 cm taller than Lucy.

**a** Work out the ratio of Lucy's height to Sam's height. Write the answer as simply as possible.

Hint: Work out Sam's height.

_____

**b** Fill in the missing fraction.

Lucy's height is _____ of Sam's height.

**c** Fill in the missing fraction.

Sam's height is _____ of Lucy's height.

**8**

Write your answers as simply as possible.

**a** Work out the ratio of red squares to white squares.

_____

**b** Write down the fraction of the squares that are white.

_____

**c** Write the missing fraction in this sentence.

The number of white squares is _____ of the number of red squares.

**1** A 500 g bag of cereal costs £6.00.

A recommended serving is 25 g.

**a** Work out the number of servings in one bag.

> Hint: Divide by 25.

_____

**b** Work out the cost of one serving.

_____

**c** Work out the cost of 100 g

_____

John buys a 500 g bag of cereal. He put 200 g in a small box and the rest in a larger box.

**d** Work out the ratio of the mass in each box. Write your ratio in its simplest form.

> Hint: Work out the mass in the larger box.

_____

**e** Write down the fraction of the cereal in the smaller box.

_____

A 380 g bag of the same cereal costs £4.18.

**f** Work out the cost of 10 g from this bag.

_____

**g** Work out the cost of 100 g from this bag.

_____

**h** Which bag is better value, 500 g or 380 g? You must show your working.

_____

_____

**2** A car in France travels 192 km and uses 12 litres of petrol.

**a** Work out the petrol consumption.
Give your answer in km/l.

> Hint: Work out 60 ÷ 12.

_____

**b** Work out the distance the car can travel with 60 litres of petrol.

_____

Petrol costs €1.32 per litre.

**c** Work out the cost of the petrol for the journey of 192 km. Give your answer in euros.

_____

The exchange rate is £1 = €1.10

**d** How many euros is £20 worth?

_____

**e** Work out the cost of the petrol for the journey of 192 km in pounds.

_____

8 km = 5 miles

**f** Convert 192 km to miles

_____

**g** Work out the fuel consumption in miles/l

_____

4.5 litres = 1 gallon

**h** Work out the fuel consumption in miles/gallon

_____

**Checklist**

I can

☐ use ratio notation

☐ write a ratio in its simplest form

☐ divide a quantity into two parts in a given ratio

☐ solve simple problems involving proportion

☐ understand the connection between fractions and ratios.

# 8 Percentages

## 8.1 One number as a percentage of another 🖩

**1** Complete these equivalent fractions.

Hint: $50 \times ? = 100$.

**a** $\dfrac{7}{50} = \dfrac{\square}{100}$ _____  **b** $\dfrac{7}{25} = \dfrac{\square}{100}$ _____

**c** $\dfrac{7}{20} = \dfrac{\square}{100}$ _____  **d** $\dfrac{7}{10} = \dfrac{\square}{100}$ _____

**2** Write these fractions as percentages.

Hint: $\dfrac{41}{50} = \dfrac{?}{100}$

**a** $\dfrac{41}{100} =$ _____  **b** $\dfrac{41}{50} =$ _____

**c** $\dfrac{22}{25} =$ _____  **d** $\dfrac{3}{10} =$ _____

**3** Write these decimals as percentages.

**a** $0.15 =$ _____ %  **b** $0.78 =$ _____ %  **c** $0.03 =$ _____ %

**4** Write the following fractions as percentages. Give your answers to the nearest whole number.

Hint: Find $2 \div 3$ with a calculator.

**a** $\dfrac{2}{3} =$ _____  **b** $\dfrac{4}{9} =$ _____

**c** $\dfrac{7}{9} =$ _____  **d** $\dfrac{3}{7} =$ _____

**5** There are 40 children. 26 are girls.

Hint: What fraction are girls?

**a** Work out the percentage of girls. _____

**b** Work out the number of boys. _____

**c** Work out the percentage of boys. _____

**6** There 180 children. 117 have brown eyes. 36 have blue eyes.

Work out the percentage with

**a** brown eyes _____ **b** blue eyes. _____

**7** There are 360 tickets for a concert. 306 are sold.

**a** What percentage are sold? _____

**b** What percentage are not sold? _____

**8** There are three candidates in an election. Here are the results.

| Candidate | Ari | Beth | Carl | Total |
|-----------|-----|------|------|-------|
| **Votes** | 63 | 42 | 27 | 132 |

Work out the percentage for each candidate. Write each answer to the nearest whole number.

Ali _____ Beth _____ Carl _____

**9** During one day 72 trains stop at a station. 57 arrive on time.

**a** Work out the percentage that are on time. Write each answer to the nearest whole number.

_____

**b** Write down the percentage that are not on time. Write your answer to the nearest whole number.

_____

# 8.2 Comparisons using percentages 🖩

Key word

percentage

**1** Jen scored the following test marks.

| Subject | Mark | Percentage |
|---------|------|------------|
| **Chinese** | 18 out of 25 | |
| **Engineering** | 132 out of 200 | |
| **Biology** | 52 out of 80 | |

Convert the marks to percentages and complete the table.

**2** **a** Ros scored 32 out of 40 in a maths test.

Write this as a percentage _____

**b** Ros scored 42 out of 60 in a science test.

Write this as a percentage _____

**c** In which subject did she score better, maths or science?_____

**3** In a school year there are 80 boys and 110 girls.

   **a** 45% of the boys have a pet.

   How many boys have a pet? _____

   **b** 44 of the girls have a pet. Show that the percentage who have a pet is smaller for girls than for boys.

_____

_____

**4** Show that 30% is more than $\frac{1}{4}$ but less than $\frac{1}{3}$.

_____

_____

**5** Dan is late for work 6 out of 48 days. Alice is late 8 out of 80 days.

   **a** Work out the percentage of days each person is late.

     Dan _____                      Alice _____

     _____                        _____

   **b** Who has better attendance? Circle your answer.      Dan      Alice

**6** This table shows the population of two towns.

| Town | 18 and under | Over 18 | Total |
|---|---|---|---|
| Alfaton | 696 | 1704 | 2400 |
| Betaville | 510 | 990 | 1500 |

   **a** Work out the percentage of the Alfaton population that is over 18.

> **Hint:** Use two numbers from each row.

_____

   **b** Show that the percentage of the population over 18 is less in Betaville than in Alfaton.

_____

**7** 275 out of 350 students at College A pass an exam.

   **a** Work out the percentage that pass. Write your answer to the nearest whole number.

_____

   155 out of 185 students at College B pass the same exam.

   **b** Show that a greater percentage pass at College B.

_____

# 8.3 Percentage change 🖩

**Key words**
increase
decrease

**1** The population of a village was 600. It increases by 25%.

   **a** Work out 25% of 600. _____

   **b** Work out the new population. _____

**2** Last June there was 40 cm of rain. This year there was 60% **less** rain.

   **a** Work out 60% of 40 cm. _____

   **b** Work out the amount of rain this year. _____

   Hint: Do a subtraction.

**3** Jak is paid £15.60 per hour. He gets a pay increase of 5%.

   **a** Work out 5% of £15.60. _____

   **b** Work out his new pay per hour. _____

**4** The cost of a car repair is £320 + VAT.

   Hint: VAT is a tax.

   The VAT rate is 20%.

   **a** Work out 20% of £320. _____

   **b** Work out the total cost including VAT. _____

**5** Last year 5600 people went to a festival. This year there are 35% fewer people.

   **a** Work out 35% of 5600. _____

   **b** Work out how many people went this year. _____

**6** The original price of a coat was £130. In a sale it is reduced by 30%.

   **a** Work out the reduction in pounds. _____

   **b** Work out the sale price. _____

**7** In a sale, prices are reduced by 25%. Complete the following table.

| Item | Original price | Reduction | Sale price |
|------|----------------|-----------|------------|
| **Chair** | £240 | £60 | |
| **Table** | £600 | | |
| **Bed** | £840 | | |
| **Cupboard** | | £90 | £270 |

**8** The price of a new car is 50% more than the price of a used car.

The price of the new car is £18 000.

Work out the price of the used car.

Hint: It is **not** £9000.

# 8 Problem solving

**1** The following table shows the marks of three students on three tests. It also shows the maximum possible mark on each test.

|  | Test A | Test B | Test C |
|---|---|---|---|
| Ali | 66 | 84 | 102 |
| Emily | 72 | 72 | 80 |
| Fran | 56 | 54 | 87 |
| Maximum mark | **80** | **120** | **150** |

**a** Show that the percentage mark for Ali on test A is 82.5%

Hint: Use Ali's mark and the maximum for test A.

**b** Work out the percentage marks for Ali on test B and test C.

Test B = _____ %                    Test C = _____ %

**c** Which test has the highest percentage for Fran? Show your working.

**d  i** Work out the maximum total mark for the 3 tests.

  **ii** Work out Emily's total mark as a percentage of the total possible.

**e** A student with an overall percentage of 70% or more is awarded a distinction.
Show that only one of these students has a distinction.

**2** The cost of renting a holiday cottage for a week in August is £625.

When you book it you pay a deposit of £100.

**a** What percentage of the cost is the deposit?

_____

**b** In October there is a 20% reduction based on the August price. Work out the cost in October.

_____

**c** At Christmas there is a 30% increase based on the August price. Work out the cost at Christmas.

_____

A couple book the cottage in August. They estimate they will spend another £800 during the week for petrol, food and entertainment.

**d** Work out the percentage of the total estimated cost of the holiday that is the cottage rent. Give your answer to the nearest whole number.

> Hint: First work out the total estimated cost.

_____

The couple actually spend less than they estimated. The rent of the cottage is 50% of the total cost.

**e** Work out the amount they actually spent on petrol, food and entertainment.

_____

**Checklist**

I can

☐ write one quantity as a percentage of another

☐ use percentages to make comparisons

☐ calculate percentage change

☐ increase or decrease an amount by a percentage.

# 9 Angles and polygons

## 9.1 Points and lines 🖩

The diagrams in this exercise are not drawn accurately. You cannot measure the angles to work out the correct answers.

**1** Work out the size of the lettered angles below.

> **Hint:** What is the sum of the angles on a straight line?

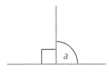     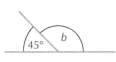     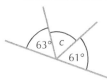

a = _____     b = _____     c = _____

**2** Calculate the size of the lettered angles below.

> **Hint:** What is the sum of the angles around a point?

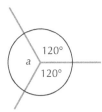     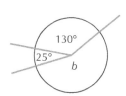     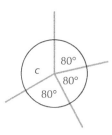

a = _____     b = _____     c = _____

**3**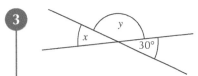

a  Write down the size of angle x. _____

b  Work out the size of angle y. _____

**4**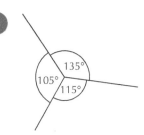

Give a reason why the angles cannot be correct.

_____

**5** Complete the following sentences. Choose the correct word or phrase from this list.

corresponding     alternate     vertically opposite

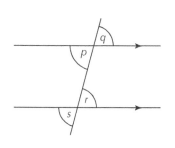

**a** $p$ and $q$ are _____ angles

**b** $p$ and $r$ are _____ angles

**c** $p$ and $s$ are _____ angles

**6** Work out the size of the lettered angles on these parallel lines.

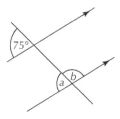

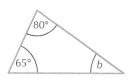

$a =$ _____     $b =$ _____     $c =$ _____     $d =$ _____

# 9.2 Triangles 🔲

The diagrams in this exercise are not drawn accurately. You cannot measure the angles to work out the correct answers.

**Key words**

isosceles

equilateral

**1** Calculate the size of the lettered angles in these diagrams.

**Hint:** What is the sum of the angles of a triangle?

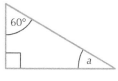

$a =$ _____

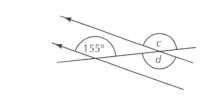

$b =$ _____

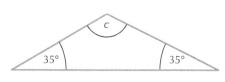

$c =$ _____

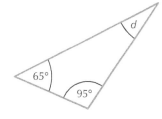

$d =$ _____

**2** Work out the value of $a$.

_____

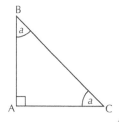

**3** Here is an equilateral triangle inside a rectangle.

Work out the size of the lettered angles.

$x =$ _____ $\qquad$ $y =$ _____

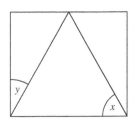

**4**

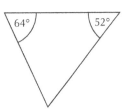

Show that this triangle is isosceles.

_____

_____

**5** PQ = PR = 10 cm. Angle Q = 57°. Work out the sizes of angle R and angle P.

$R =$ _____ $\qquad$ $P =$ _____

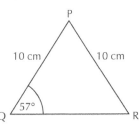

**6** One angle of an isosceles triangle is 130°. Work out the size of the other two angles. You must show your working.

_____

**7** Work out the size of angle $a$ and angle $b$.

$a =$ _____ $\qquad$ $b =$ _____

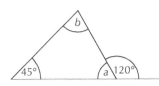

# 9.3 Quadrilaterals and other polygons 🖩

**Key words**

quadrilateral

polygon

interior angle

The diagrams in this exercise are not drawn accurately. You cannot measure the angles to work out the correct answers.

**1** Complete this sentence.

The four angles of a quadrilateral add up to _____.

**2** Work out the size of the lettered angles.

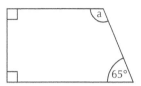

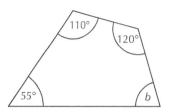

$a =$ _____

$b =$ _____

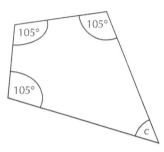

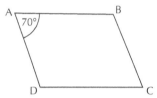

$c =$ _____

$d =$ _____

**3** ABCD is a parallelogram.

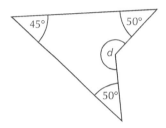

**a** Write down the size of angle C. _____

**b** Work out the size of angle D. _____

**4**

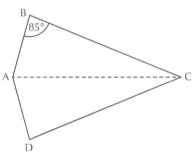

AC is a line of symmetry.

**a** Circle the name of this shape.

    kite                parallelogram            rhombus            trapezium

**b** Write down the size of angle D. _____

**c** Angle A = 150°. Work out the size of angle C. _____

**5** QR and PS are parallel.

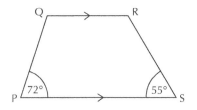

**a** Circle the name of this shape.

kite            parallelogram

rhombus         trapezium

**b** Angle P = 72°. Work out the size of angle Q. _____

**c** Angle S = 55°. Work out the size of angle R. _____

**6** A rectangle is removed from a square to make this shape.

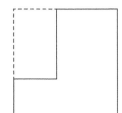

**a** Circle the name of the shape.

pentagon        hexagon        octagon        quadrilateral

**b** Work out the sum of the interior angles of the shape.

> Hint: One angle is different from all the others.

_____

**7** This shape is made from a rectangle and an equilateral triangle.

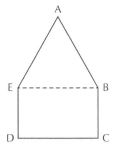

**a** Circle the name of the shape.

pentagon        hexagon        octagon        quadrilateral

**b** Work out the size of angle E. _____

**c** Work out the sum of all of the interior angles. _____

## 9.4 Shapes on coordinate axes ✗

**Key words**

symmetry

vertex

**1**

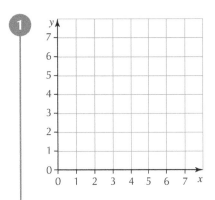

ABCD is a rectangle.

**a** Plot the points A(2, 2) , B(6, 2) and C(6, 4).

**b** Draw the rectangle.

**c** Write down the coordinates of D. _____

**d** The rectangle has two lines of symmetry. Write down their equations.

_____

**2** PQRS is a parallelogram.

**a** Plot P(2, 3), Q(2, 6) and R(5, 3).

**b** Draw PQ and QR.

**c** Complete the parallelogram.

**d** Write down the coordinates of S. _____

**e** Work out the size of the interior angles of the parallelogram.

_____

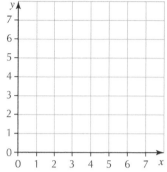

**3** **a** Draw the line $y = 4$.

**b** Plot A(1, 4), B(3, 6) and C(7, 4).
ABCD is a kite and $y = 4$ is the
line of symmetry of the kite.

**c** Draw the kite.

**d** Write down the coordinates of D. _____

**e** Work out the size of angle BAD.

_____

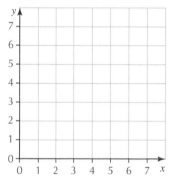

**4** **a** Plot A(4, 0) and C(4, 6).
A and C are opposite vertices of the square ABCD.

**b** Draw the square.

> **Hint:** Start with the centre of the square.

**c** Write down the coordinates of B and D.

_____

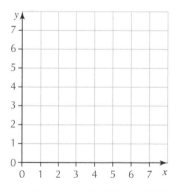

**5** (4, 3) is the centre of a square. One vertex is at (3, 0).

**a** Plot (4, 3) and (3, 0).

**b** Draw the square.

> **Hint:** Start with the vertex opposite (3, 0).

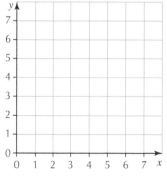

**6**

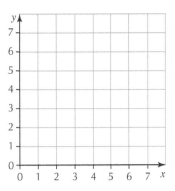

**a** Draw the line $y = x$.

ABCDEF is a hexagon.

Hint: It is a diagonal line.

**b** Plot A(2, 2), B(1, 4), C(3, 6) and D(5, 5).

$y = x$ is a line of symmetry of the hexagon.

**c** Draw the hexagon.

Hint: Draw the reflection of the points you know.

**d** There is another line of symmetry. Write down its equation. _____

# 9 Problem solving

**1** This question is about the following two triangles.

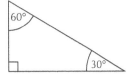 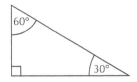 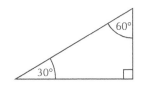

You can also reflect them like this.

**a** Put the two triangles together to make a rectangle.

Hint: Join two edges together.

**b** Put the two triangles together to make an equilateral triangle.

**c** Put the two triangles together to make an isosceles triangle.

**d** Write down the sizes of the interior angles of the isosceles triangle.

_____

**e** Put the two triangles together to make a parallelogram.

**f** Write down the sizes of the interior angles of the parallelogram. _____

**g** Put the two triangles together to make a kite.

**h** Write down the sizes of the interior angles of the kite. _____

**2**

Hint: Look at the angles at P.

This pattern is made from regular hexagons.

**a** How many hexagons meet at point P?

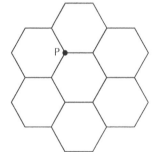

_____

**b** Explain why the angles of a regular hexagon must be 120°.

_____

This pattern also contains regular hexagons.

**c** How many shapes meet at Q?

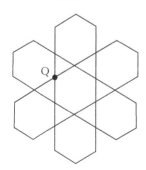

_____

**d** Explain why the triangles must be equilateral.

_____

_____

This pattern also contains regular hexagons.

**e** Write down the name of the other shape in the pattern.

_____

**f** Work out the angles of the other shape.

_____

Here is a regular octagon divided into smaller shapes.

**g** Work out the size of each angle of the regular octagon. Explain how you know.

_____

_____

**Checklist**

I can

- [ ] work out angles on a straight line
- [ ] work out angles round a point
- [ ] work out angles in parallel lines
- [ ] work out angles in a triangle
- [ ] work out angles in a quadrilateral
- [ ] name different types of polygons.

# 10 Perimeter, area and volume

## 10.1 Perimeter and area

**1** Work out the perimeter of each shape.

> **Hint:** Perimeter = length of the boundary.

**a**
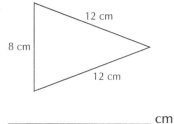

_____ cm

**b**
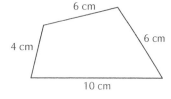

_____ cm

**2** Work out the perimeter of each rectangle.

**a**

_____ cm

**b**

_____ m

**3** Work out the area of each rectangle in question 2.

**a** _____ cm²      **b** _____ m²

**4** The perimeter of a square is 20 cm.
**a** Work out the length of each side.

_____

**b** Work out the area of the square.

_____

**5**

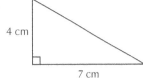

10 cm

5 cm

This is a rectangle.

**a** Work out the area of the rectangle.

_____

**b** Work out the area of the triangle. **Hint:** What fraction of the rectangle is the triangle?

_____

**6** Work out the area of each triangle.

**a**

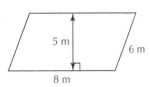

4 cm

7 cm

**b**

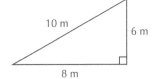

10 m

6 m

8 m

_____ cm²        _____ m²

**7** Work out the perimeter of each of these parallelograms.

**a**

5 m

6 m

8 m

**b**

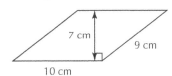

7 cm

9 cm

10 cm

_____ m        _____ cm

**8** Work out the **area** of each of the parallelograms in question 7. **Hint:** Area = base × height.

**a** _____ m²        **b** _____ cm²

**9** This shape is made from two rectangles.

All lengths are in centimetres.

**a** Work out the perimeter of the shape.

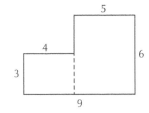

5

4

6

3

9

_____

**b** Work out the area of the shape. **Hint:** Work out the area of each rectangle separately.

_____

**10** Here is an L-shape.

All lengths are in centimetres.

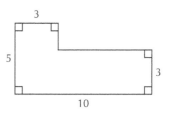

**a** Work out the perimeter of the shape.

_____

**b** Work out the area of the shape.

_____

# 10.2 Circles

**Key words**

circumference

area

**1**

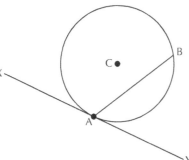

C is the centre of the circle.

**a** Circle the correct name for the straight line AB.

diameter       chord       sector       tangent

**b** Circle the correct name for the straight line XAY.

diameter       chord       sector       tangent

**2**

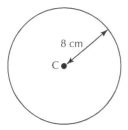

C is the centre of the circle.

**a** Work out the diameter of the circle.

_____

**b** Calculate the circumference. Give your answer to the nearest centimetre.

_____

**3** C is the centre of the circle.

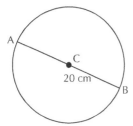

AB = 20 cm.

Calculate the circumference. Give your answer to the nearest centimetre.

_____

**4** The circumference of a circle is 1 m.

Work out the diameter to the nearest centimetre. Circle the correct answer.

8 cm          1 cm          32 cm          50 cm

**5** Calculate the circumference of each of these circles. Give your answers to the nearest centimetre.

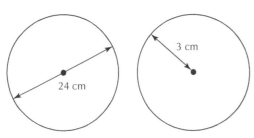

**a** _____ cm   **b** _____ cm

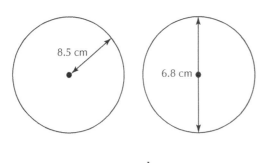

**c** _____ cm   **d** _____ cm

**6**

5 cm

The radius of this circle is 5 cm.

Calculate the area of the circle.

Give your answer to the nearest whole number.

Show your working.

_____

**7** Calculate the area of each of the circles in question **5**.

**a** _____ cm²          **b** _____ cm²

**c** _____ cm²          **d** _____ cm²

**8**

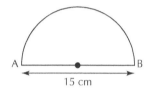

A                    B

15 cm

This shape is half a circle.

**a** Calculate the length of the arc AB, to the nearest centimetre.

> Hint: An arc is part of the circumference.

_____

**b** Calculate the area of the sector, to the nearest cm².

_____

## 10.3 Solids

**1**

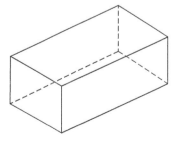

This is a cuboid. Write down the number of

**a** faces _____ **b** edges _____ **c** vertices. _____

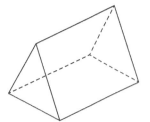

**2**

This is a triangular prism. Write down the number of

**a** faces _____ **b** edges _____ **c** vertices. _____

**3**

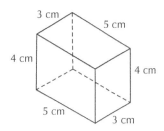

This is a cuboid. Work out the area of

**a** the largest face _____ **b** the smallest face. _____

**4**

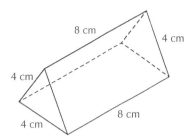

This is a triangular prism.
Work out the area of one of the rectangular faces.

_____

**5**

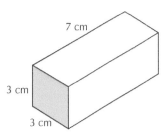

The coloured face of this cuboid is a square. Work out

**a** the area of the square _____ cm² **b** the volume of the cuboid. _____ cm³

**6** Calculate the volume of each of these cuboids.

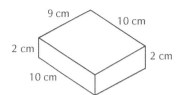

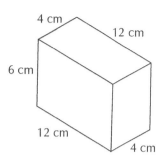

**a** _____ cm³          **b** _____ cm³

**7**

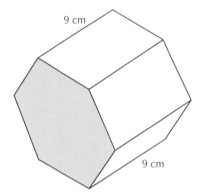

This is a hexagonal prism.

**a** Write down the number of

  **i** faces _____   **ii** edges _____   **iii** vertices. _____

**b** The area of the coloured end is 30 cm². The length is 9 cm. Calculate the volume.

_____

_____

**8** Each edge of a cube is 8 cm. Calculate

**a** the area of one face _____ cm²

**b** the volume. _____ cm³

# 10 Problem solving

**1** This is a rectangular tile T.

**a** Work out the perimeter of the tile.

6 cm

4 cm   T

_____

**b** Work out the area of the tile.

_____

Two tiles can be put together to make a larger rectangle as shown.

**c** Work out the perimeter of the larger rectangle.

_____

| T |
|---|
| T |

**d** Work out the area of the larger rectangle.

_____

**e** Show how two of the tiles can be put together to make a different rectangle.

> Hint: Your drawing does not need to use the accurate measurements.

**f** For the rectangle in part **e** work out

  **i** the perimeter _____  **ii** the area. _____

**g** Draw a different rectangular tile that has the same **area** as tile T. Write the lengths of the sides on your diagram.

**h** Work out the perimeter of the tile in part **g**.

_____

**i** A square tile has the same perimeter as tile T. Work out the area of the square tile.

_____

_____

**2** This is a cube. Each edge has length 3 cm.

**a** Work out the area of one face.

_____

3 cm   3 cm

3 cm

**b** Work out the total area of all the faces.

> Hint: There are 6 faces.

_____

**c** Work out the volume of the cube.

_____

**d** Work out the total length of all the edges.

Hint: There are 12 edges.

_____

Two cubes are put together to make a cuboid.

**e** Work out the volume of the cuboid.

_____

**f** Work out the area of one rectangular face of the cuboid.

_____

**g** Work out the total area of all the faces of the cuboid.

_____

**h** Work out the total length of all the edges.

_____

10 cubes

10 cubes are put in a line to make a long cuboid.

**i** Work out the total length of all the edges.

_____

**Checklist**

I can

☐ work out the perimeter of a shape

☐ work out the area of a rectangle, a triangle and a parallelogram

☐ work out the circumference and area of a circle

☐ find the number of vertices, faces and edges on a simple solid

☐ work out the volume of a cuboid.

# 11 Transformations

## 11.1 Reflections

**Key words**

reflection

image

**1** Draw the reflection of each shape in the mirror line.

a

b

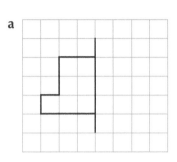

**2** Draw the reflection of each shape in the mirror line.

a

b

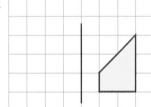

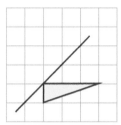

**3**

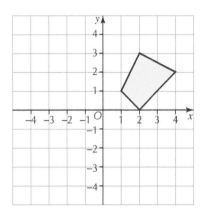

a Draw the reflection of the triangle in the *x*-axis. Label it A.

b Draw the reflection of the triangle in the *y*-axis. Label it B.

**4**

a Draw the reflection of the quadrilateral in the *x*-axis. Label it A.

b Draw the reflection of the quadrilateral in the *y*-axis. Label it B.

**5**

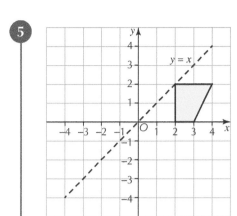

a  Draw the reflection of the shape in the x-axis. Label it A.

b  Draw the reflection of the shape in the y-axis. Label it B.

c  Draw the reflection of the shape in line y = x. Label it C.

Hint:  The line y = x is drawn for you.

**6**

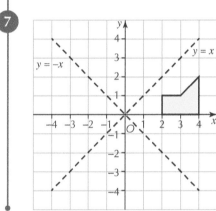

a  Draw the reflection of the shape in the line x = 3. Label it A.

b  Draw the line y = 3.

c  Draw the reflection of the shape in the y = 3. Label it B.

**7**

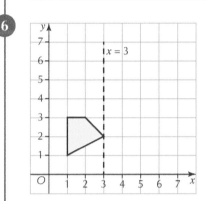

a  Draw the reflection of the shape in line y = x. Label it A.

b  Draw the reflection of the shape in line y = − x. Label it B.

Hint:  The line is on the grid.

## 11.2 Translations and rotations

**1**

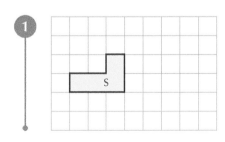

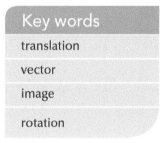

Key words

translation

vector

image

rotation

**a** $\begin{pmatrix} 4 \\ 2 \end{pmatrix}$ means 4 squares to the right and 2 squares up

Translate S by the vector $\begin{pmatrix} 4 \\ 2 \end{pmatrix}$. Label the image A.

**b** $\begin{pmatrix} 4 \\ -2 \end{pmatrix}$ means 4 squares to the right and 2 squares down

Translate S by the vector $\begin{pmatrix} 4 \\ -2 \end{pmatrix}$. Label the image B.

**c** Write down the vector for the translation from B to A.

_____

**2**

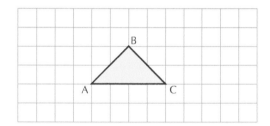

Write down the vectors for these translations.

**a** D to B _____ **b** B to A _____ **c** A to C _____

**3** Rotate triangle ABC

**a** 180° about A

**b** 180° about B

**c** 180° about C.

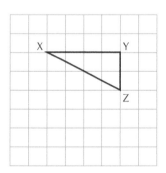

**4** **a** Rotate the triangle 90° clockwise about X.

**b** Rotate the triangle 90° anticlockwise about Z.

**5**
a Translate P by the vector $\begin{pmatrix} -2 \\ 3 \end{pmatrix}$.

b Rotate P 180° about (0, 0).

c Rotate P 90° clockwise about (0, 0).

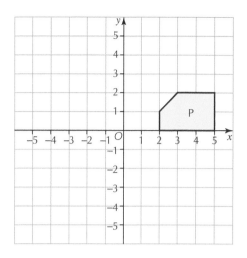

**6**
a Rotate R 90° clockwise about (0, 0). Label the image S.

b Rotate S 90° clockwise about (0, 0). Label the image T.

c Translate R by the vector $\begin{pmatrix} -4 \\ -2 \end{pmatrix}$. Label the image U.

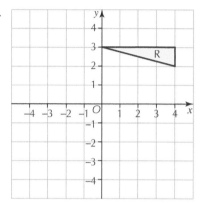

**7**
a Rotate T 180° about (5, 5). Label the image U.

Hint: (5, 5) is one of the vertices of the triangle.

b Rotate T 180° about (5, 3). Label the image V.

c Write down the vector for the translation from U to V.

d Translate T by the vector $\begin{pmatrix} -1 \\ -3 \end{pmatrix}$. Label the image W.

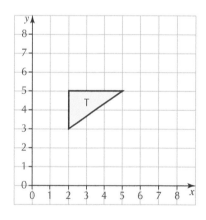

## 11.3 Enlargements

Key words
enlargement
scale factor
centre

**1**

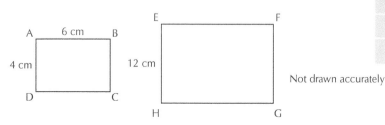

A — 6 cm — B
4 cm
D — C

E — F
12 cm
H — G

Not drawn accurately

ABCD is a rectangle. EFGH is an enlargement of rectangle ABCD.

**a** Work out the scale factor of the enlargement. _____

**b** Work out the length EF. _____

**2**

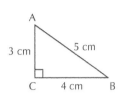 

Not drawn accurately

Triangle ABC is enlarged to triangle DEF.

**a** Work out the scale factor of the enlargement. _____

**b** Work out the perimeter of triangle DEF. _____

**3** The perimeter of this shape is 30 cm.

It is enlarged with a scale factor of 6.

Work out the perimeter of the enlargement. _____

**4** EFGH is an enlargement of ABCD.

The scale factor is 2.

O is the centre of the enlargement.

EF has been drawn. Complete the enlargement of EFGH.

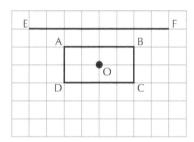

**5** One side of an enlargement of this triangle has been drawn.

The centre is X. The scale factor is 3.

Complete the enlargement.

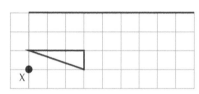

**6** Draw an enlargement of this square, centre (0, 0), scale factor 2.

Hint: Double the coordinates of the vertices.

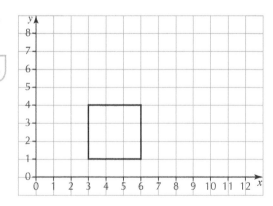

**7** Draw an enlargement of this rhombus, centre (0, 0), scale factor 3.

Hint: Multiply the coordinates of the vertices by 3.

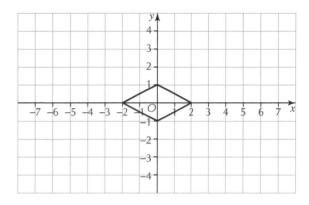

**8** Draw an enlargement of this triangle, centre (0, 0), scale factor 2.

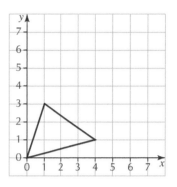

# 11 Problem solving

**1**  **a** Reflect triangle A in the *x*-axis. Label the image B.

Hint: The image is the new triangle.

**b** Reflect triangle A in the *y*-axis. Label the image C.

**c** Rotate triangle A 180° about (0, 0). Label the image D.

**d** Reflect triangle E in the *y*-axis. Label the image F.

**e** Rotate triangle E 180° about (0, 0). Label the image G.

**f** Reflect triangle E in the *x*-axis. Label the image H.

**g** Describe the transformation that maps triangle E to triangle A.

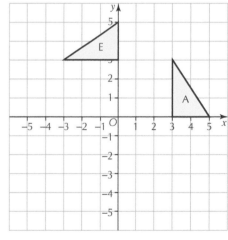

_____

**h** Translate triangle E by the vector $\begin{pmatrix} 0 \\ -6 \end{pmatrix}$. Label the image J.

**i** Describe the transformation that maps triangle J to triangle H.

_____

**2**

**a** Draw the enlargement of triangle A, centre X, scale factor 2.

Two vertices of the enlargement have been drawn on the grid. Label the enlargement B.

**b** Draw the enlargement of triangle B, centre X, scale factor 2. Label it C.

The longest side of A has length 6 cm.

**c** Work out the length of the longest side of triangle B.

_____

**d** Work out the length of the longest side of triangle C.

_____

**e** Triangle C is an enlargement of triangle A.

Work out the scale factor of the enlargement. _____

**f** On your drawing, show that triangle B can be divided into triangles the same size and shape as triangle A.

The area of triangle A is 9 cm².

**g** Work out the area of triangle B. _____

**h** Work out the area of triangle C. _____

---

**Checklist**

I can

☐ draw the reflection of a shape

☐ rotate a shape 90° or 180° about a given centre

☐ translate a shape by a given vector

☐ enlarge a shape with a given scale factor

☐ describe different types of transformations.

# 12 Probability

## 12.1 Relative frequency 🖩

**1** A drawing pin is dropped 20 times. It lands point up or point down.

| Point | Up | Down | Total |
|---|---|---|---|
| **Frequency** | 13 | 7 | 20 |

Write down the relative frequency of

**a** point up _____

**b** point down. _____

> Hint: Relative frequency = $\dfrac{\text{number of favourable events}}{\text{total number of events}}$.

**2** Two coins are spun together 50 times. Here are the results.

| Outcome | 2 heads | 2 tails | 1 head, 1 tail |
|---|---|---|---|
| **Frequency** | 9 | 14 | 27 |

Work out the relative frequency of

**a** 2 heads _____

**b** the same on both coins. _____

**3** Vehicles travelling along a road in one hour are recorded.

| Vehicle | Car | Van | Lorry |
|---|---|---|---|
| **Frequency** | 154 | 32 | 14 |

**a** Work out the total number of vehicles.

_____

**b** Work out each of these relative frequencies. Write your answers as percentages.

**i** car _____  **ii** lorry _____  **iii** not a lorry _____

**4** Ahmed throws a dice 20 times. Here are his scores.

2  3  1  5  5  4  5  1  3  2  5  3  6  2  4  6  5  2  3  3

**a** Complete the table of his scores.

| Score | 1 | 2 | 3 | 4 | 5 | 6 | Total |
|---|---|---|---|---|---|---|---|
| **Frequency** | 2 | 4 | 5 | | | | 20 |

**b** Work out the relative frequencies of each of these results. Give your answers as decimals.

**i** 2 _____  **ii** 6 _____  **iii** an odd number _____

**5** A computer simulation throws two dice 1000 times.

The frequency of a total of 8 or more is 427.

   **a** Work out the relative frequency of a total of less than 8.

_____

The relative frequency of double 6 is 0.04.

   **b** Work out the frequency of double 6.

> **Hint:** Frequency = relative frequency × total number of times the two dice are thrown.

_____

**6** A survey of 200 people records age and gender as shown in the following table.

| | Under 18 | 18–60 | Over 60 | Total |
|---|---|---|---|---|
| **Male** | 12 | 42 | 26 | 80 |
| **Female** | 20 | 75 | 25 | 120 |
| **Total** | 32 | 117 | 51 | 200 |

   **a** Work out the relative frequency of females.

_____

   **b** For females only, work out the relative frequency of under 18s.

_____

   **c** For under 18s only, work out the relative frequency of females.

_____

# 12.2 Calculating probabilities

**Key words**

random

fair

equally likely

**1** Here are eight number cards. One is chosen at random.

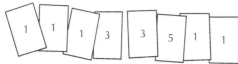

Put a letter on the probability scale below for each of the outcomes.

**A:** the card is 1      **B:** the card is less than 5      **C:** the card is an even number

0                                              1

**2** Carla throws an ordinary fair dice. Work out the probability she throws

   **a** 2 _____      **b** more than 2 _____      **c** an odd number. _____

**3** 15 men, 30 women and 5 children each buy one raffle ticket. There is one prize.

Work out the probability that the winner is

**a** a woman _____     **b** not a woman _____     **c** not a child. _____

**4** There are 10 balls in a box, 4 red, 3 blue, 2 green and 1 yellow.

A ball is taken out at random.

**a** Work out the probability that the ball is

    **i** red _____     **ii** blue or green _____     **iii** not yellow. _____

The yellow ball is taken from the box.

A second ball is taken at random from the box.

**b** Work out the probability that the second ball is

    **i** red _____     **ii** blue or green _____     **iii** not yellow. _____

**5** Sam catches the bus each day for 60 days. He records how late it is.

| | On time | Up to 5 minutes late | 5 to 10 minutes late | Over 10 minutes late |
|---|---|---|---|---|
| Frequency | 40 | 10 | 6 | 4 |

Use the table to find the probability that the bus will be

**a** on time _____     **b** late _____     **c** at least 5 minutes late._____

**6** The probability that Carrie beats Darren at badminton is 0.3.

They play 20 games. How many can Carrie expect to win?

> Hint: Expected number of wins = probability of win × number of games played.

_____

**7** A spinner has three sections of different sizes and colours.

Here are the results of 25 spins.

| Colour | Green | Blue | Red | Total |
|---|---|---|---|---|
| Frequency | 5 | 12 | 8 | 25 |

**a** Use the results to write the probability of each colour.

    **i** green _____     **ii** blue _____     **iii** red _____

**b** The spinner is spun 120 times. Work out the expected number of greens.

> Hint: Expected number of greens = probability of green × total number of spins.

# 12.3 Possibility spaces ✗

**Key words**

possibility

outcome

**1** In a café there are three choices of main courses:
pie (A), risotto (B), pasta (C).

There are two choices of puddings: fruit (X), yogurt (Y).

Jon chooses a main and a pudding. One possible choice is AX.

**a** List the other possible choices in the same way.

_____

A third pudding is added to the list: ice cream (Z). There is no risotto left.

**b** List all the possible choices now.

_____

**2** An ordinary fair dice is thrown and a fair coin is spun.

**a** Complete this table of outcomes.

|  |  | **Dice** |  |  |  |  |  |
|---|---|---|---|---|---|---|---|
|  |  | **1** | **2** | **3** | **4** | **5** | **6** |
| **Coin** | **Head (H)** | 1H |  |  |  |  |  |
|  | **Tail (T)** |  | 2T |  |  |  |  |

**b** Write down the number of different outcomes.

_____

**c** Work out the probability that Sonia throws

**i** 2 and a tail _____   **ii** an even number and a head. _____

**3** This spinner has three equal sectors red (R), yellow (Y) and blue (B).

**a** The arrow is spun twice. Complete this table of possible outcomes.

|  |  | **First spin** |  |  |
|---|---|---|---|---|
|  |  | **Red (R)** | **Yellow (Y)** | **Blue (B)** |
| **Second spin** | **Red (R)** |  |  |  |
|  | **Yellow (Y)** |  |  | BY |
|  | **Blue (B)** | RB |  |  |

**b** Write down the number of possible outcomes.

_____

**c** Work out the probability of

**i** 2 reds _____

**ii** the same colour on each spin _____

**iii** different colours on each spin. _____

**4** An ordinary fair dice is thrown twice. Here is a possibility space diagram.

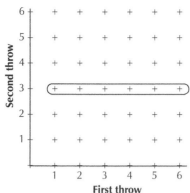

**a** Write down the number of outcomes.

_____

The loop shows the event '3 on the second throw'.

**b** Work out the probability of three on the second throw.

_____

**c** Work out the probability of

   **i** 6 on both throws _____

   **ii** the same number on both throws _____

   **iii** an even number on both throws _____

   **iv** at least one 6. _____

**5** Two ordinary fair dice are thrown. The scores are added.

**a** Complete this table of possible totals.

**First dice**

|  |  | 1 | 2 | 3 | 4 | 5 | 6 |
|---|---|---|---|---|---|---|---|
| | 6 | | | | | 11 | |
| | 5 | | | | | | |
| **Second** | 4 | | | | 8 | | |
| **dice** | 3 | | | | | | |
| | 2 | 3 | | | | | |
| | 1 | | | | | | |

**b** Write down the most likely total.

_____

**c** Write down the least likely totals.         Hint: There are two possible answers.

_____

**d** Work out the probability of a total of

   **i** 12 _____        **ii** 3 _____

   **iii** 8 _____        **iv** 10 or more. _____

**1** A spinner has 5 equal sectors.

The arrow is spun 20 times.

Here are the results.

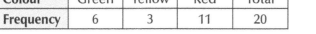

| Colour | Green | Yellow | Red | Total |
|---|---|---|---|---|
| Frequency | 6 | 3 | 11 | 20 |

**a** Work out the relative frequency of each colour as a decimal.

> Hint: Write it as a fraction first.

**i** green _____  **ii** yellow _____  **iii** red _____

The arrow is now spun 30 more times.

Here are the results.

| Colour | Green | Yellow | Red | Total |
|---|---|---|---|---|
| Frequency | 7 | 6 | 17 | 30 |

**b** Combine the results of all 50 spins into a single table.

| Colour | Green | Yellow | Red | Total |
|---|---|---|---|---|
| Frequency |  |  |  | 50 |

**c** Work out the following relative frequencies for the combined results, writing your answers as decimals.

**i** green _____  **ii** yellow _____  **iii** red _____

**d** Assume the spinner is fair. Write the probability of each colour as a decimal.

**i** green _____  **ii** yellow _____  **iii** red _____

**e** Tom says "The spinner is not fair because the relative frequencies and the probabilities are different".

Do you agree?          Yes          No

Give a reason for your answer.

_____

**2** Two fair coins are spun.

This outcome is HT.

**a** Complete this table to show all the possible outcomes.

**Coin 1**

|  |  | Head (H) | Tail (T) |
|---|---|---|---|
| **Coin 2** | **Head (H)** |  |  |
|  | **Tail (T)** | HT |  |

**b** Work out the probability of

  **i** 2 heads _____

  **ii** 1 head and 1 tail. _____

> Hint: The answer to part **ii** is not $\frac{1}{4}$

Now **three** fair coins are spun.

This outcome is HTT.

**c** Complete this table to show all the possible outcomes.

<table>
<tr><td colspan="2"></td><td colspan="4" align="center">Coins 1 and 2</td></tr>
<tr><td colspan="2"></td><td>HH</td><td>HT</td><td>TH</td><td>TT</td></tr>
<tr><td rowspan="2">Coin 3</td><td>Head (H)</td><td></td><td></td><td></td><td>TTH</td></tr>
<tr><td>Tail (T)</td><td></td><td>HTT</td><td></td><td></td></tr>
</table>

**d** Work out the probability of

  **i** 3 heads _____

  **ii** 2 heads and 1 tail _____

  **iii** 1 heads and 2 tails _____

Now four coins are spun.

**e** Complete this table to show all the possible outcomes.

<table>
<tr><td colspan="2"></td><td colspan="8" align="center">Coins 1, 2 and 3</td></tr>
<tr><td colspan="2"></td><td>HHH</td><td></td><td></td><td></td><td></td><td></td><td></td><td></td></tr>
<tr><td rowspan="2">Coin 4</td><td>Head (H)</td><td></td><td></td><td></td><td></td><td></td><td></td><td></td><td></td></tr>
<tr><td>Tail (T)</td><td>HHHT</td><td></td><td></td><td></td><td></td><td></td><td></td><td></td></tr>
</table>

**f** Work out the probability of

  **i** 4 heads _____

  **ii** 3 heads and 1 tail _____

  **iii** 2 heads and 2 tails. _____

**Checklist**

I can

☐ list outcomes systematically

☐ work out relative frequencies

☐ work out probabilities based on equally likely outcomes

☐ use tables and probability spaces for combined outcomes.

# 13 Statistics

## 13.1 Tables, charts and diagrams

**Key words**

pictogram

bar chart

pie chart

**1** Monty is comparing car insurance prices.

There are two types of car insurance: comprehensive and third party.

Here are the prices for four companies.

| Company | Comprehensive | Third Party |
|---------|---------------|-------------|
| A | £280 | £225 |
| B | £324 | £247 |
| C | £295 | £219 |
| D | £307 | £253 |

**a** Which company is most expensive for comprehensive insurance?

_____

**b** Which company is cheapest for third party insurance?

_____

**c** Work out the difference between the two prices for company D.

_____

**2** This pictogram shows the number of calls to a telephone helpline.

**Telephone calls to helpline**

Monday    ◯ ◯ ◯ ◯

Tuesday   ◯ ◯ ◖

Wednesday

There were 40 calls on Monday.

**a** Work out the number of calls on Tuesday.

_____

**b** There were 15 calls on Wednesday. Show this on the pictogram.

_____

**3** This bar chart shows the populations of six countries in Europe.

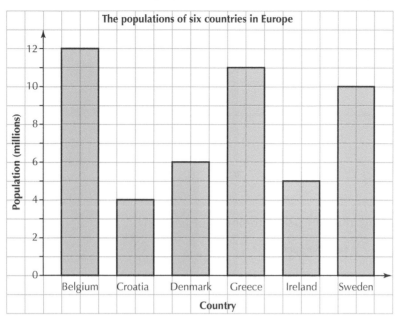

**a** Write down the country with the largest population.

_____

**b** Work out the difference between the populations of Greece and Ireland.

_____

**c** Work out the total population of the six countries.

_____

**4** This graph shows the average temperature in Paris each month.

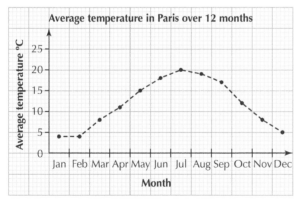

**a** Name the coldest months.

_____

**b** Name the month with an average temperature of 15°C.

_____

**c** Work out the number of months with an average temperature below 15°C.

_____

**5** New Zealand won 18 medals at the 2016 Olympics.
How many medals were

**New Zealand medals at the 2016 Olympics**

**a** silver _____

**b** gold _____

**c** bronze. _____

# 13.2 Calculating statistics 🖩

| Key words |
| --- |
| mode |
| median |
| range |
| mean |
| frequency table |

**1** A group of students were asked their favourite sport.

**Favourite Sports**

**Favourite Sports**

Write down the modal favourite sport for

> **Hint:** The mode is the most common.

**a** girls _____          **b** boys. _____

**2** Here are 25 ages in years.

| 11 | 12 | 12 | 13 | 13 | 13 | 13 | 14 | 14 | 15 | 15 | 15 | 15 | 15 | 16 |

| 16 | 17 | 17 | 17 | 17 | 17 | 17 | 18 | 20 | 20 |

Work out

**a** the modal age _____    **b** the median _____    **c** the range. _____

**3** Here are the hourly rates of pay for 9 people.

£8.50    £8.50    £8.50    £9.30    £9.30    £10.15    £10.80    £12.40    £14.80

**a** Work out

   **i**  the median _____        **ii**  the range. _____

Two more people are added to the list. They both have hourly rates of £12.25.

**b** For all 11 people work out

   **i**  the median _____        **ii**  the range. _____

**4** Here are the number of children in 40 families.

0 0 0 0 0 0 1 1 1 1 1 1 1 1 1 1 1 1 1 2 2

2 2 2 2 2 2 2 3 3 3 3 3 3 3 4 4 5 5 5 7

a  Complete the following frequency table.

| Number of children | 0 | 1 | 2 | 3 | 4 | 5 | 6 | 7 |
|---|---|---|---|---|---|---|---|---|
| Frequency | 6 | 12 | 9 | | | | | |

b  Work out

   i  the mode _____    ii  the median _____    iii  the range. _____

**5** Here are the times five people wait in a queue.

3 minutes    7 minutes    2 minutes    10 minutes    2 minute

a  Work out the range.

_____

b  Work out the mean waiting time in minutes.

_____

**6** Here are the marks for six students for two exam papers.

| Student | Ali | Beth | Carl | Dima | Ethan | Finn |
|---|---|---|---|---|---|---|
| Paper 1 | 28 | 29 | 41 | 18 | 30 | 29 |
| Paper 2 | 24 | 30 | 33 | 28 | 41 | 36 |

a  Work out the range for Paper 1.

_____

b  Work out the mean mark for Carl.

_____

c  Work out the mean mark for Paper 2.

_____

**7** Here are the number of hours of sunshine each day in one week in Seatown.

| Day | Sun | Mon | Tue | Wed | Thu | Fri | Sat |
|---|---|---|---|---|---|---|---|
| Hours | 2 | 2 | 4 | 7 | 8 | 8 | 4 |

a  Work out

   i  the range _____    ii  the median _____    iii  the mean. _____

In Lakeside the mean amount of sunshine in the same week was 3 hours a day.

b  Work out the total number of hours sunshine in Lakeside.

_____

# 13 Problem solving

**1** The following bar chart shows the energy content of 5 types of baked goods.

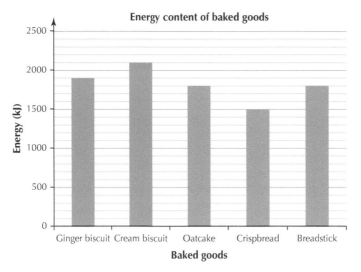

Hint: Energy is measured in kJ.

**a** Write down the energy content of ginger biscuits _____ kJ

**b** Write down the type of baked good with the least energy content.

_____

**c** Work out the difference in energy content between oatcakes and crispbread.

_____ kJ

This chart shows the protein and fat content of 4 types of baked goods.

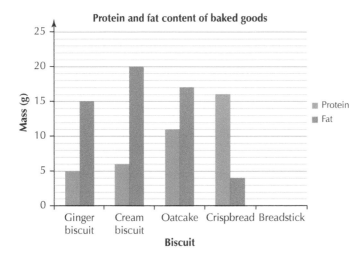

**d** Breadsticks have 14 g of protein and 9 g of fat. Add these to the chart.

**e** Work out the median protein content.

_____ g

**f** Work out the range of the fat content.

_____ g

This pie chart shows the carbohydrate content of the baked goods.

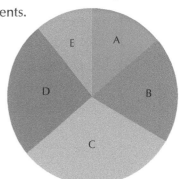

**g** Write the correct letter (A, B, C, D or E) after these statements.

  **i** The largest carbohydrate content is ginger biscuits,

  letter _____

  **ii** The smallest carbohydrate content is oatcake,

  letter _____

  **iii** The median carbohydrate content is crispbread,

  letter _____

**2** Five people each carried out three tasks. Here are their times in minutes.

|  | Ian | Joe | Kim | Lisa | Mika |
|---|---|---|---|---|---|
| **Task 1** | 12 | 18 | 20 | 14 | 11 |
| **Task 2** | 16 | 14 | 13 | 22 | 17 |
| **Task 3** | 21 | 23 | 18 | 15 | 18 |

**a** Work out the median time for task 1.

_____

**b** Work out the range for task 2.

_____

**c** Work out the mean time for task 3.

_____

**d** Work out the mean time for the three tasks for Kim.

_____

40 people carry out task 4. Here are their times in minutes.

8  8  8  8  8  8  9  9  9  9  9  10  10  11  11  11  11  11  11  12
12  12  12  12  13  13  13  13  13  14  14  14  14  14  14  14  14  14
14  14

**e** Complete the following frequency table for Task 4.

| Time (minutes) | 8 | 9 | 10 | 11 | 12 | 13 | 14 |
|---|---|---|---|---|---|---|---|
| Frequency | 6 | 5 |  | 6 |  |  | 11 |

**f** For Task 4 work out

  **i** the range _____    **ii** the modal time _____    **iii** the median time. _____

**g** All the times for Task 4 add up to 458 minutes. Work out the mean time for Task 4.

_____

100 people do Task 5. The total of all their times is 875 minutes.

**h** On average, which task was completed more quickly?

Circle your answer.　　Task 4　　　　Task 5

Give a reason for your answer.

_____

**Checklist**

I can

☐ interpret and draw charts and diagrams

☐ interpret and construct frequency tables

☐ work out the median, mode and mean for a set of data

☐ work out the range of a set of data.

# Glossary

**24-hour clock:** Measuring the time based on all 24 hours of the day.

**Alternate (angles):** Angles that lie on either side of a line that cuts a pair of parallel lines; the line forms two pairs of alternate angles and the angles in each pair are equal.

**Angle:** The space between two straight lines that diverge from a common point or between two planes that extend from a common line.

**Area:** The extent of a two-dimensional surface enclosed within a specified boundary or geometric figure.

**Axis:** One of the two lines on a graph on which the scales of measurement are marked.

**Bar chart:** A diagram which is a series of bars or blocks of the same width to show frequencies.

**Bracket:** A pair of marks that are placed around a series of symbols in a mathematical expression to indicate that those symbols function as one item within the expression.

**Centre:** The midpoint of any line or figure, especially the point within a circle or sphere that is equidistant from any point on the circumference or surface; a point, area, or part that is approximately in the middle of a larger area or volume; the point, axis or pivot about which a body rotates.

**Circumference:** The perimeter of a circle; every point on the circumference is the same distance from the centre, and this distance is the radius.

**Common factor:** A whole number that divides exactly into two or more numbers; 2 is a common factor of 6, 8 and 10.

**Common multiple:** An integer or polynomial that is a multiple of each integer or polynomial in a group.

**Coordinates:** The two sets of numbers or letters on a map or graph that you need in order the find that point.

**Corresponding (angles):** Angles that lie on the same side of a pair of parallel lines cut by a line; the line forms four pairs of corresponding angles, and the angles in each pair are equal.

**Cube:** A solid having six plane square faces in which the angle between two adjacent sides is a right angle.

**Cube numbers:** A number that can be obtained by multiplying together three of the same number.

**Cube root:** A number that makes another number when it is multiplied by itself twice. For example, the cube root of 8 is 2 since $2 \times 2 \times 2 = 8$.

**Cuboid:** A solid shape with six rectangular surfaces or four rectangular and two square surfaces.

**Decimal place:** the position of a digit after the decimal point, each successive position to the right having a denominator of an increased power of ten.

**Decrease:** To become less in quantity, size or intensity.

**Denominator:** The bottom number in a fraction.

**Edge:** The line where two faces or surfaces of a 3D shape meet.

**Enlargement:** A transformation in which the object is enlarged to form an image.

**Equally likely:** The outcomes of an event are equally likely when each has the same probability of occurring. For example, when tossing a fair coin the outcomes 'heads' and 'tails' are equally likely.

**Equation:** A relation in which two expressions are separated by an equals sign with one or more variables. An equation can be solved to find one or more answers, but it may not be true for all values of $x$.

**Equilateral (triangle):** A triangle in which all the sides are equal and all the angles are 60°.

**Equivalent fraction:** Any fraction that can be made equal to another fraction by cancelling. For example $\dfrac{9}{12} = \dfrac{3}{4}$.

**Expression:** A collection of numbers, letters, symbols and operators representing a number or amount; for example, $x^2 - 3x + 4$.

**Face:** The area on a 3D shape enclosed by edges.

**Factor:** A number that divides exactly (no remainder) into another number; for example, the factors of 12 are {1, 2, 3, 4, 6, 12}.

**Fair:** All outcomes are equally likely.

**Formula:** A mathematical rule, using numbers and letters, which shows a relationship between variables; for example, the conversion formula from temperatures in Fahrenheit to temperatures in Celsius is: $C = \dfrac{5}{9}(F - 32)$.

**Fraction:** A number that can be expressed as a proportion of two whole numbers.

**Frequency:** The number of times each value occurs.

**Frequency table:** A table that shows all the frequencies after all the data has been collected.

**Gradient:** The slope of a line; the vertical difference between the coordinates divided by the horizontal difference.

**Image:** The result of a reflection or other transformation of an object.

**Improper fraction:** A fraction that has a numerator greater than the denominator.

**Increase:** To make or to become greater in size, degree, frequency, etc; to grow or expand.

**Index (notation):** Expressing a number in terms of one or more of its factors, each expressed as a power.

**Intercept:** The point where a line cuts or crosses an axis.

**Interior angle:** The inside angle between two adjacent sides of a 2D shape, at a vertex.

**Isosceles (triangle):** A triangle in which two sides are equal and the angles opposite the equal sides are also equal.

**Litre:** A metric unit of volume that is a thousand cubic centimetres. It is equal to 1.76 British pints.

**Mean:** A number that is the average of a set of numbers.

**Median:** The middle value in a frequency distribution, below and above which lie values with equal total frequencies.

**Midpoint:** The point on a line that is at an equal distance from either end.

**Mixed number:** A number made up of a whole number and a fraction, for example $3\frac{3}{4}$.

**Mode:** The value in a range of values that has the highest frequency as determined statistically.

**Multiple:** Any member of the times table; for example multiples of 7 are 7, 14, 21, 28, etc.

***n*th term:** An expression in terms of $n$ where $n$ is the position of the term; it allows you to find any term in a sequence, without having to use a term-to-term rule.

**Numerator:** The top number in a fraction.

**Opposite (side):** The side that is the furthest away from a given angle, in a right-angled triangle.

**Outcome:** A possible result of an event in a probability experiment, such as the different scores when throwing a dice.

**Parallelogram:** A four sided shape where both pairs of opposite sides are parallel.

**Pattern:** Numbers or objects that are arranged to follow a rule.

**Percentage:** Any fraction or decimal expressed as an equivalent fraction with a denominator of 100 but written with a percentage sign (%), for example $0.4 = \frac{40}{100} = 40\%, \frac{4}{25} = \frac{16}{100} = 16\%$.

**Perimeter:** The curve or line enclosing a plane area; the length of this curve or line.

**Pictogram:** A frequency table where the frequency for each type of data is shown by a symbol.

**Pie chart:** A method of comparing discrete data. A circle is divided into sectors whose angles each represent a proportion of the whole sample.

**Polygon:** A closed 2D shape with straight sides.

**Power:** The number of times you use a number or expression in a repeated multiplication; it is written as a small raised number; for example, $2^2$ is 2 multiplied by itself, and $2^2 = 2 \times 2$ and $4^3 = 4 \times 4 \times 4$.

**Possibility:** The likelihood of something happening from a range of choices.

**Prime (number):** A number with only two factors, 1 and itself.

**Prism:** A 3D shape that has the same cross-section wherever it is cut perpendicular to its length.

**Proportion:** 1) A relationship that maintains a constant ratio between two variable quantities. 2) A relationship between four numbers or quantities in which the ratio of the first pair equals the ratio of the second pair.

**Quadratic:** Having terms involving one or two variables and a constant, such as $x^2 - 3$ or $y^2 + 2y + 4$, where the highest power of the variable is two.

**Quadrilateral:** A polygon having four sides.

**Random:** Chosen by chance, without selection; every item has an equal chance of being chosen.

**Range:** The difference between the highest and lowest values for a set of data.

**Ratio:** The ratio of A to B is a number found by dividing A by B. It is written as A:B. For example, the ratio of 1 m to 1 cm is written as 1 m : 1 cm = 100 : 1. Notice that the two quantities must both be in the same units if they are to be compared in this way.

**Reflection:** The image formed when a 2D shape is reflected in a mirror line or line of symmetry; the process of reflecting an object.

**Relative frequency:** An estimate for the theoretical probability.

**Rotation:** A turn about a central point, called the centre of rotation.

**Scale:** The number of squares that are used for each unit on an axis.

**Scale factor:** The ratio of the distance on the image to the distance it represents on the object; the number that tells you how much a shape is to be enlarged.

**Sequence:** A pattern of numbers that are related by a rule.

**Significant figure:** In the number 12 068, 1 is the first and most significant figure and 8 is the fifth and least significant figure. In 0.246, the first and most significant figure is 2. Zeros at the beginning or end of a number are not significant figures.

**Simplify:** To make an equation or expression easier to work with or understand by combining like terms or cancelling; for example, $4a - 2a + 5b + 2b = 2a + 7b, \frac{12}{18} = \frac{2}{3}, 5:10 = 1:2$.

**Solve:** To work out the answer to a problem or to obtain the roots of an equation.

**Speed:** The rate at which an object moves; for example, the speed of the car was 40 miles per hour.

**Square:** A shape with four sides that are all the same length and four corners that are all right angles.

**Square numbers:** A number formed when any integer is multiplied by itself. For example, $3 \times 3 = 9$ so 9 is a square number.

**Square root:** A number that produces a specified quantity when multiplied by itself. For example, the square root of 16 is 4. Not all square roots are whole numbers. It uses the symbol $\sqrt{}$, so $\sqrt{25} = 5$, and $\sqrt{7} = 2.645,751...$.

**Standard form:** A way of writing a number as $a \times 10^n$, where $1 \leq a < 10$ and $n$ is a positive or negative integer.

**Substitute:** Replace a variable in an expression with a number and work out the value; for example, if you substitute 4 for $t$ in $3t + 5$ the answer is 17 because $3 \times 4 + 5 = 17$.

**Symmetry:** An exact correspondence in position or form about a given point, line or plane.

**Term:** 1) A part of an expression, equation or formula. Terms are separated by + and – signs. 2) A number in a sequence or pattern.

**Term-to-term:** The rule that shows what to do to one term in a sequence to work out the next term.

**Translation:** A movement along, up, down or diagonally on a coordinate grid.

**Triangle:** An object, arrangement or flat shape with three straight sides and three angles.

**Triangle numbers:** All numbers that can be arranged in an equilateral triangular pattern.

**Vector:** A quantity such as velocity that has magnitude and acts in a specific direction.

**Vertex:** The point at which two lines meet in a 2D or 3D shape.

**Vertices:** The plural of vertex.

# Notes

Notes

# Answers

## 1.1 Multiples

**1** 45, 50, 55

**2** 42, 49, 56

**3** even numbers

**4** 11, 22, 33, 44, 55, 66

**5** 20, 40, 60, 80, 100, 120, 140

**6** 21, 24, 27, 30, 33, 36, 39

**7** Any multiple of 20, e.g. 20, 40, 60, 80, 100, …

**8** **a** A circle round 90, 93, 96, 99
   **b** a square round 92, 96, 100
   **c** 96

**9** **a** 4, 8, 12, 16, 20, 24   **b** 6, 12, 18, 24, 30, 36
   **c** Any multiples of 12, e.g. 12, 24, …

**10** **a** 15, 30, 45, 60, 75, 90
   **b** 10, 20, 30, 40, 50, 60, 70, 80, 90
   **c** 30, 60, 90   **d** 30

**11** Any five multiples of 6, e.g. 6, 12, 18, 24, 30, …

## 1.2 Factors

**1** 1, 15, 3, 5

**2** 1, 2, 4, 5, 10, 20

**3** 50 and 20

**4** **a** 1, 2, 4   **b** 1, 2, 3, 4, 6   **c** 1, 3, 5   **d** 1

**5** **a** 1, 2, 3, 6, 9, 18   **b** 1, 3, 9, 27   **c** 1, 3, 9

**6** **a** 1, 2, 4, 8, 16   **b** 1, 2, 4, 7, 14, 28   **c** 1, 2, 4

**7** Any three from 1, 2, 5, 10

**8** 11

## 1.3 Prime numbers

**1** **a** 10, 12, 14, 16, 18, 20 crossed out
   **b** 11, 13, 17, 19 circled

**2** **a** **i** 1, 21, 3, 7   **ii** 1, 22, 2, 11   **iii** 1, 23   **iv** 1, 5, 25
   **b** 23

**3** 23 and 29

**4** 89

**5** Each number has a factor other than 1 and the number itself,
   **a** e.g. even number so 2 is a factor
   **b** e.g. 5 is a factor since the last digit is 5
   **c** e.g. 9 is a factor since $9 \times 111 = 999$

**6** $5 \times 7$ (or $7 \times 5$)

**7** **a** $2 \times 13$   **b** $3 \times 11$   **c** $5 \times 13$

**8** **a** 12   **b** 70   **c** 110   **d** 125

**9** **a** 20   **b** 140

**10** **a** $2 \times 3 \times 3$   **b** $7 \times 11$
   **c** $2 \times 3 \times 5$   **d** $2 \times 2 \times 2 \times 2 \times 2$

## 1.4 Lowest common multiple and highest common factor

**1** **a** 6, 12, 18, 24, 30, 36   **b** 4, 8, 12, 16, 20, 24
   **c** 12 and 24   **d** 12

**2** **a** 10   **b** 20   **c** 30   **d** 10

**3** 12

**4** 50

**5** **a** 1, 2, 3, 4, 6, 12   **b** 1, 2, 3, 6, 9, 18
   **c** 1, 2, 3, 6   **d** 6

**6** **a** 1, 2, 5, 10   **b** 10

**7** **a** 20   **b** $\frac{2}{5}$

**8** 15

## 1 Problem solving

**1** **a** 10 is a factor of 60 since $10 \times 6 = 60$
   **b** 8 is not a factor of 60; $7 \times 8 = 56$ so 7 rows would have 4 chairs left over.
   **c** **i** 12 rows. The highest factor less than 14 is 12 because $12 \times 5 = 60$.
   **ii** 5 rows (12 chairs in each row)

**2** **a** $7 + 7$ and $3 + 11$   **b** $5 + 19$, $7 + 17$ and $11 + 13$
   **c** 11 is a prime number and $385 = 35 \times 11$ or $385 \div 11 = 35$
   **d** 5 and 7 are prime factors; $5 \times 77 = 7 \times 55 = 385$
   **e** 1, 385, 35, 55 and 77

# ANSWERS TO CHAPTER 2: FRACTIONS, DECIMALS AND PERCENTAGES

## 2.1 Equivalent fractions

**1** a $\frac{3}{6} = \frac{1}{2}$  b $\frac{12}{16} = \frac{3}{4}$  c $\frac{4}{12} = \frac{1}{3}$

**2** a $\frac{1}{4}$  b $\frac{2}{5}$  c $\frac{2}{3}$  d $\frac{1}{2}$

**3** a $\frac{1}{2} = \frac{3}{6}$  b $\frac{3}{5} = \frac{6}{10}$  c $\frac{1}{2} = \frac{6}{12}$  d $\frac{6}{8} = \frac{3}{4}$

  e $\frac{3}{2} = \frac{6}{4}$  f $\frac{2}{3} = \frac{8}{12}$  g $\frac{3}{4} = \frac{9}{12}$  h $\frac{5}{2} = \frac{15}{6}$

**4** Possible answers include $\frac{3}{4}, \frac{6}{8}, \frac{12}{16}, \frac{15}{20}, \frac{18}{24}$

**5** a $\frac{1}{2}$  b $\frac{1}{3}$  c $\frac{1}{4}$  d $\frac{3}{4}$

**6** a $\frac{2}{3}$  b $\frac{5}{8}$  c $\frac{2}{5}$  d $\frac{3}{4}$

**7** a 1  b $\frac{3}{5}$  c $\frac{1}{2}$  d $\frac{2}{5}$

  e 1  f $\frac{5}{4}$ or $1\frac{1}{4}$

**8** b $1\frac{1}{4}$  c $2\frac{1}{4}$  d $1\frac{1}{2}$  e $3\frac{1}{2}$

  f $1\frac{3}{8}$  g $2\frac{1}{8}$  h $1\frac{7}{10}$  i $3\frac{3}{10}$

**9** a $\frac{11}{2}$  b $\frac{13}{4}$  c $\frac{19}{8}$  d $\frac{17}{3}$

**10** $\frac{2}{5}$  $\frac{1}{2}$  $\frac{2}{3}$  $\frac{3}{4}$

## 2.2 Arithmetic with fractions

**1** a $\frac{6}{8}$  b $\frac{7}{8}$

**2** a $\frac{3}{9}$  b $\frac{5}{9}$

**3** a $\frac{1}{4} + \frac{2}{4} = \frac{3}{4}$  b $\frac{1}{8} + \frac{6}{8} = \frac{7}{8}$

  c $\frac{1}{6} + \frac{3}{6} = \frac{4}{6} = \frac{2}{3}$  d $\frac{5}{10} + \frac{1}{10} = \frac{6}{10} = \frac{3}{5}$

**4** a $\frac{2}{4} = \frac{1}{2}$  b $\frac{3}{8}$  c $\frac{5}{8}$

  d $\frac{7}{8}$  e $\frac{6}{10} = \frac{3}{5}$  f $\frac{8}{10} = \frac{4}{5}$

**5** a $\frac{1}{3}$  b $\frac{3}{5}$  c $\frac{5}{10} = \frac{1}{2}$

  d $\frac{8}{10} = \frac{4}{5}$  e $\frac{6}{8} = \frac{3}{4}$  f $\frac{2}{8} = \frac{1}{4}$

**6** a $\frac{1}{4}$  b $\frac{3}{8}$  c $\frac{3}{8}$  d $\frac{3}{8}$  e $\frac{4}{10}$  f $\frac{2}{10}$

**7** b $3\frac{1}{2}$  c $1\frac{1}{4}$  d $3\frac{3}{4}$  e 2  f $3\frac{1}{5}$

**8** a $2\frac{1}{3}$  b $2\frac{2}{3}$  c $4\frac{1}{2}$  d $2\frac{2}{5}$  e $2\frac{1}{4}$  f $3\frac{1}{2}$

**9**

| × | $\frac{1}{4}$ | $\frac{1}{3}$ | $\frac{1}{2}$ | $\frac{2}{3}$ | $\frac{3}{4}$ |
|---|---|---|---|---|---|
| **3** | $\frac{3}{4}$ | 1 | $1\frac{1}{2}$ | 2 | $2\frac{1}{4}$ |
| **5** | $1\frac{1}{4}$ | $1\frac{2}{3}$ | $2\frac{1}{2}$ | $3\frac{1}{3}$ | $3\frac{3}{4}$ |

## 2.3 Fractions and decimals

**1** a 0.25  b 0.75  c 2.5  d 5.25

**2** a 0.3  b 0.9  c 1.1  d 2.7

**3** a $\frac{2}{5}$  b $\frac{4}{5}$  c $\frac{3}{5}$  d $1\frac{1}{5}$

**4** a $\frac{3}{20}$  b $\frac{7}{20}$  c $\frac{9}{20}$  d $3\frac{11}{20}$

**5** a 0.375  b 0.625  c 0.875

**6** A = 1.2 = $1\frac{1}{5}$    B = 1.8 = $1\frac{4}{5}$

  C = 2.3 = $2\frac{3}{10}$    D = 2.6 = $2\frac{3}{5}$

**7** a 8.3  b 4.25  c 6.6  d 5.125

**8** a $9\frac{7}{10}$  b $12\frac{4}{5}$  c $10\frac{3}{4}$  d $8\frac{1}{8}$

**9** a $1\frac{1}{5} = 1.2$  b $1\frac{3}{5} = 1.6$  c $3\frac{3}{4} = 3.75$  d $5\frac{1}{4} = 5.25$

**10** a 0.666…  b 0.111…  c 0.555…

**11** $\frac{5}{8}$  $\frac{2}{3}$  $\frac{7}{10}$  $\frac{4}{5}$

## 2.4 Percentages

**1** 63% and 90%

**2** a 0.44  b 0.4  c 0.04

**3**

| 0.5 | 0.35 | 0.77 | 0.6 | 0.8 | 0.06 |
|---|---|---|---|---|---|
| 50% | 35% | 77% | 60% | 80% | 6% |

**4**

| 25% | 70% | 5% | 75% | 90% | 15% |
|---|---|---|---|---|---|
| $\frac{1}{4}$ | $\frac{7}{10}$ | $\frac{1}{20}$ | $\frac{3}{4}$ | $\frac{9}{10}$ | $\frac{3}{20}$ |

**5** 15%

**6** $\frac{1}{4} + \frac{1}{5} = \frac{9}{20}$

**7** a £5  b £2  c £14  d £15  e £4  f £16

**8 a** $\frac{1}{5}$

**b i** £3 **ii** £8 **iii** 50p or £0.50
**iv** 11 kg **v** 7 cm **vi** 16 m

**9**

| £7.50 | £30 | £37.50 | £60 | £150 |
|-------|-----|--------|-----|------|
| £4 | £16 | £20 | £32 | £80 |

## 2.5 Working with fractions and percentages

**1 a** 10 kg **b** 12 m **c** 45 people
**d** 36 kg **e** 25 g **f** 21 m

**2 a** $\frac{1}{5}$ **b** 20%

**3 a i** $\frac{3}{4}$ **ii** $\frac{3}{10}$ **iii** $\frac{3}{5}$ **b i** 75% **ii** 30% **iii** 60%

**4 a** 0.32 **b i** £64 **ii** £38.40 **iii** £8 **iv** £1.92

**5 a i** 0.08 **ii** 0.45

**b**

| £2 | £3.20 | £4 | £19.20 |
|----|-------|----|--------|
| £11.25 | £18 | £22.50 | £108 |

**6 a** £6 **b** £66 **c** £54

**7 a** £32 **b** £112 **c** £48

**8 a** 6 kg **b** 126 kg **c** 114 kg

**9** e.g. 4% of £650 = 0.04 × £650 = £26; £650 + £26 = £676

## 2 Problem solving

**1 a** $\frac{3}{5}$ **b** 15 **c** 45%

**d** 60% of 90 = 54, **e** 54 − 18 = 36 more

**2 a i** £3 **ii** 25%

**b i** 40% of £80 = £32 so the sale price is £80 − £32 = £48

**ii** No. 40% of £210 = £84. The price with a 40% reduction is £210 − £84 = £126

# ANSWERS TO CHAPTER 3: WORKING WITH NUMBERS

## 3.1 Order of operations

**1 a** 11 **b** 20 **c** 8 **d** 12 **e** 11 **f** 29
**2 a** 12 **b** 2 **c** 5 **d** 50 **e** 25 **f** 6
**3 a** 10 **b** 4 **c** 1 **d** 2 **e** 12 **f** 5
**4 a** F 14 **b** F 6 **c** T **d** T **e** T **f** T
**g** F 5 **h** T **i** F 2 **j** F 2

**5** He did the subtraction first. He should do the multiplication first. The answer is 6.

**6** Two possible answers are 5 + 3 × 4 and 1 + 2 × 8.

**7 a** 25 **b** 2 **c** 60

## 3.2 Powers and roots

**1 a** 9 **b** 49 **c** 100
**2 a** 41 **b** 85
**3 a** 1.69 **b** 12.25 **c** 21.16
**4 a** 6 **b** 9 **c** 12 **d** 15 **e** 30 **f** 32
**5 a** 1.4 **b** 3.1 **c** 8.4
**6 a** 125 **b** 8 **c** 216 **d** 1000
**7 a** 1.331 **b** 17.576 **c** 531.441
**8 a** 2 **b** 5 **c** 10 **d** 8
**9 a** 16 **b** 256 **c** 64
**10** $3^4 = 81$ and $4^3 = 64$ and so $3^4$ is larger
**11** $3^2, 2^4, 4^3$

## 3.3 Rounding numbers

**1 a** 40 **b** 680 **c** 250
**2 a** 400 **b** 3600 **c** 3100
**3 a** 4000 **b** 6000 **c** 19 000
**4 a** 43 **b** 52 **c** 2 **d** 4
**e** 12 **f** 15 **g** 3 **h** 81
**i** 99 **j** 67 **k** 13 **l** 9
**5 b** 6.8 **c** 8.9 **d** 14.5 **e** 11.6
**f** 58.5 **g** 8.6 **h** 3.8
**6 a** 8.7 **b** 11.4 **c** 14.2
**7 a** 4.67 **b** 3.34 **c** 8.88 **d** 2.24
**e** 7.21 **f** 9.49
**8 a** 0.67 **b** 0.17 **c** 0.83
**9 a** 800 **b** 400 **c** 6000
**d** 7000 **e** 5000 **f** 60 000

## 3.4 Standard form

**1 a** 100 **b** 1000 **c** 100 000
**2 a** $10^3$ **b** $10^4$ **c** $10^6$
**3 a** 150 **b** 2400 **c** 38 000
**4 a** 73 **b** 580 **c** 2900
**5 a** 100 **b** 100 **c** 1000
**6 a** $3.2 \times 10^3$ **b** $6 \times 10^3$ **c** $1.23 \times 10^3$
**7 a** $4 \times 10^4$ **b** $7.3 \times 10^4$ **c** $2.6 \times 10^5$
**d** $8.03 \times 10^5$ **e** $7 \times 10^6$ **f** $4.8 \times 10^6$
**8 a** 900 **b** 920 **c** 300 000
**d** 1 800 000 **e** 475 000 **f** 14 100
**9** B C A D
**10 a** $5.1 \times 10^5$ **b** $3.3 \times 10^5$

## 3.5 Units

**1 a** 25 **b** 45 **c** 60 **d** 50
**2** 1.65 m
**3** 74 kg
**4** 45 minutes
**5 a** 2000 **b** 1500 **c** 250
**6 a** cm **b** ml or l **c** kg
**d** km **e** g **f** m

**7 a** 9     **b** 400     **c** 2000
   **d** 50     **e** 500     **f** 53

**8 a** 3500     **b** 4650     **c** 350

**9 a** 6500     **b** 2850     **c** 610

**10 a** 18 : 20     **b** 14 : 05

## 3 Problem solving

**1 a** 5 and 4 in that order

   **b** One pair is 2 and 4. The other pair is 3 and 5. The order does not matter.

   **c** One pair is 2 and 3. The other pair is 4 and 5. The answer is 26.

   **d** One pair is 2 and 5. The other pair is 3 and 4 to make 49

**2 a** 126 000, 288 000     **b** 90 000 , 100 000, 300 000
   **c** $5.02 \times 10^5$

# ANSWERS TO CHAPTER 4: SEQUENCES OF NUMBERS

## 4.1 Describing a sequence

**1 a** 16     **b** 19     **c** 26
   **d** 13     **e** 51     **f** 40

**2 a** 25, 28, 31, 34

   **b** Add 3 to the last number to get the next

**3 a** 27     **b** 52     **c** 64
   **d** 26     **e** 56     **f** 24

**4 a** add 5     **b** add 7     **c** subtract 2     **d** subtract 4

**5 a** 13 and 18     **b** 33

**6 a** multiply by 2     **b** multiply by 3
   **c** multiply by 5     **d** multiply by 4

**7** 10, 20, 40

**8 a** 52     **b** subtract 12

## 4.2 Recognising sequences

**1 a** 16, 25, 36     **b** 64, 100

**2** 25, 49, 81, 121

**3 a** 5, 7, 9, 11    **b** odd numbers adding 2 each time

**4** 64, 125, 216

**5** $10 \times 10 \times 10 = 1000$

**6 a** $1 + 2 + 3 + 4 = 10$     **b** 15     **c** 21     **d** 55

**7** $8 \times 8 = 64$ and $4 \times 4 \times 4 = 64$

## 4.3 The *n*th term of a sequence

**1 a** 5     **b** 9     **c** 1     **d** 14

**2 a** 6     **b** 12     **c** 15     **d** 30

**3 a** 8     **b** 13     **c** 3     **d** 10

**4** bottom line 6, 8, 10, 12, 14

**5** bottom line 4, 6, 8, 10, 12

**6 a** 1     **b** 10     **c** 13     **d** 28

**7** 7, 9, 11, 13

**8** 1, 4, 7, 10

**9**
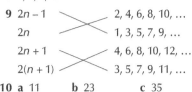

**10 a** 11     **b** 23     **c** 35

**11 a** 11, 21, 31, 41, 51     **b** 101

## 4 Problem solving

**1 a** 1, 3, 5, 7, 9     **b i** 4    **ii** 8    **iii** 12    **iv** 16

   **c** The first four multiples of 4

   **d** 1, 3, 6, 10, 15     **e i** 4    **ii** 9    **iii** 16    **iv** 25

   **f** square numbers     **g i** 36    **ii** 100

**2 a** dots 4, 6, 8, 10     **b** 14
   **c** lines 4, 7, 10, 13     **d** 22
   **e** If $n = 4$ then $3 \times 4 + 1 = 13$    **f** 61

# ANSWERS TO CHAPTER 5: COORDINATES AND GRAPHS

## 5.1 Coordinates

**1 a** A (3, 2)    C (−3, −4)    D (3, −4)
   **b** Point (0, 2) marked on the diagram
   **c** (3, −1) (−3, −1) (0, −4)

**2 a and b**

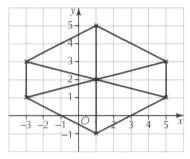

   **c** (1, 2)

**3 a and b**

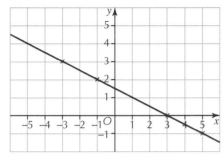

**c** (0, 1.5)

**4 a–d**

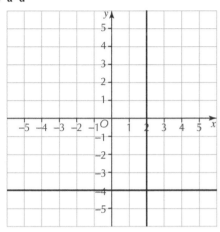

**e** (2, −4)

## 5.2 The equation of a straight line

**1 a** B $x = 5$, C $x = −4$    **b** E $y = −3$, F $y = 3$

**2 a i** 2    **ii** 1    **iii** −2

**b**

| x | 2 | 0 | −2 | −4 |
|---|---|---|----|----|
| y = x + 3 | 5 | 3 | 1 | −1 |

**c and d**

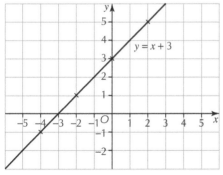

**e** Possible answers are (1, 4) or (−1, 2) or (−3, 0) or (−5, −2)

**3 a i** −4    **ii** −6    **iii** −10

**b**

| x | −2 | −1 | 0 | 1 | 2 |
|---|----|----|---|---|---|
| y = 2x | −4 | −2 | 0 | 2 | 4 |

**c and d**

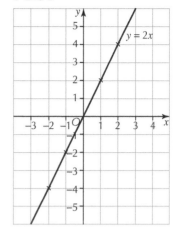

**e** Possible answers are (0.5, 1) or (1.5, 3) or (−1.5, − 3)

**4 a i** 3    **ii** 1    **iii** 4    **iv** −1

**b**

| x | −1 | 0 | 1 | 2 | 3 | 4 | 5 |
|---|----|---|---|---|---|---|---|
| y | 5 | 4 | 3 | 2 | 1 | 0 | −1 |

**c**

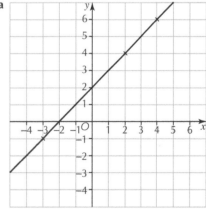

## 5.3 Intercept and gradient

**1 a**

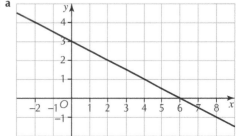

**b** (0, 2) and (−2, 0)

**2 a**

**b** Circle (4, 1) and (8, –1)

**3 a** 4    **b** $\dfrac{1}{3}$

**4 a** 3    **b** $\dfrac{1}{2}$    **c** $\dfrac{1}{5}$

**5 a**

| $x$ | $-2$ | $-1$ | $0$ | $1$ | $2$ | $3$ |
|---|---|---|---|---|---|---|
| $y = 2x + 4$ | 0 | 2 | 4 | 6 | 8 | 10 |

**b**

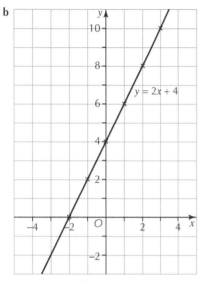

**c i** (0, 4)    **ii** 2

## 5.4 Quadratic graphs

**1 a**

| $x$ | $0$ | $1$ | $2$ | $3$ | $4$ | $5$ |
|---|---|---|---|---|---|---|
| $y = x^2$ | 0 | 1 | 4 | 9 | 16 | 25 |

**b and**

**c**

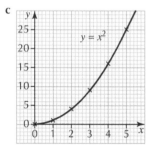

**2 a**

| $x$ | $0$ | $1$ | $2$ | $3$ | $4$ |
|---|---|---|---|---|---|
| $y = x^2 + 4$ | 4 | 5 | 8 | 13 | 20 |

**b and c**

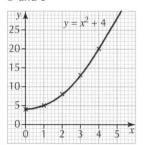

**3 a**

| $x$ | $0$ | $1$ | $2$ | $3$ | $4$ | $5$ |
|---|---|---|---|---|---|---|
| $y = x^2 - 10$ | $-10$ | $-9$ | $-6$ | $-1$ | 6 | 15 |

**b**

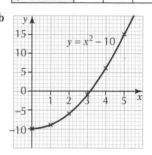

**4 a i** 4    **ii** 16

**b**

| $x$ | $-4$ | $-3$ | $-2$ | $-1$ | $0$ | $1$ | $2$ | $3$ | $4$ |
|---|---|---|---|---|---|---|---|---|---|
| $y = x^2$ | 16 | 9 | 4 | 1 | 0 | 1 | 4 | 9 | 16 |

**c**

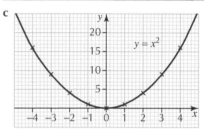

## 5 Problem solving

**1 a and e**

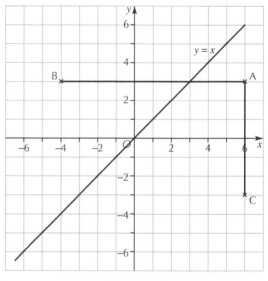

**b** (1, 3)    **c** (6, 0)    **d** $y = 3$    **f** (3, 3)    **g** (−4, −3)

**2 a**

| $x$ | $0$ | $1$ | $2$ | $3$ |
|---|---|---|---|---|
| $3x$ | 0 | 3 | 6 | 9 |

**b, e and i**

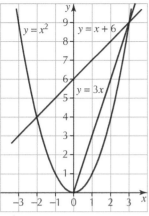

$y = x^2$  $y = x + 6$  $y = 3x$

**c** 3

**d**

| $x$ | $-3$ | $-2$ | $-1$ | $0$ | $1$ | $2$ | $3$ |
|---|---|---|---|---|---|---|---|
| $x + 6$ | 3 | 4 | 5 | 6 | 7 | 8 | 9 |

**f** 1  **g** (0, 6)

**h**

| $x$ | $-3$ | $-2$ | $-1$ | $0$ | $1$ | $2$ | $3$ |
|---|---|---|---|---|---|---|---|
| $x^2$ | 9 | 4 | 1 | 0 | 1 | 4 | 9 |

**j** (3, 9)

# ANSWERS TO CHAPTER 6: EXPRESSIONS AND EQUATIONS

## 6.1 Substituting into formulae

**1 b** $R + 4$   **c** $2R$   **d** $\frac{1}{2}R$ or $R \div 2$

**2 a** 15   **b** 1   **c** 3
   **d** $-2$   **e** 12   **f** 30

**3 b** $20 - 12 = 8$   **c** $40 + 18 = 58$   **d** $2 + 3 = 5$
   **e** $2 \times 10 = 20$   **f** $5 \times 2 = 10$

**4 a** 12 m   **b** 18 m

**5 a** 12 cm   **b** 27 m

**6 a** £50   **b** £90

**7 a** 20 cm²   **b** 80 cm²

## 6.2 Simplifying expressions

**1 a** $5x$   **b** $2y$   **c** $8p$   **d** $5t$

**2 a** $2t + 3$   **b** $4x$   **c** $2 + 3k$   **d** $4n - 3$

**3** $3t + 4$

**4 a** $2x + 2$   **b** $3y - 6$   **c** $4a + 12$   **d** $10a - 5$

**5 a** $4x + 4y$   **b** $3a + 6b$

**6**
$4(x + 2)$ — $2x + 8$
$2(x + 4)$ — $2x + 8$
$8(x + 1)$ — $8x + 8$
$2(4x + 1)$ — $8x + 2$
$4(2x + 1)$ — $8x + 4$, $4x + 8$

**7 a** $2(c + 5)$   **b** $3(x - 3)$   **c** $2(w + 5)$   **d** $2(4n - 1)$
**8 a** $4(a + b)$   **b** $6(x - 2y)$   **c** $10(2s + 3t)$   **d** $4(a + 2b - 3c)$

## 6.3 Solving equations

**1 a** $x = 15$   **b** $y = 7$
**2 a** $t = 4$   **b** $y = 6$
**3 a** $g = 11$   **b** $r = 12$
**4 a** $p = 6$   **b** $T = 18$
**5 a** $x = 4$   **b** $y = 8$
**6 a** $y = 4$   **b** $x = 8$   **c** $w = 7$   **d** $g = 4$   **e** $m = 30$

## 6 Problem solving

**1 a** $L + L + L + L = 4L$   **b** $6L$
   **c** $(6L + 12)$ or $6(L + 2)$
**2 a** 12   **b** 9, 18   **c** 7, 24   **d** 15, 20

# ANSWERS TO CHAPTER 7: RATIO AND PROPORTION

## 7.1 Ratio notation

**1** 16

**2 a** $7 : 4$   **b** $4 : 7$

**3** $2 : 1$

**4 a** 3   **b** 3

**5 b** $3 : 1$   **c** $4 : 1$   **d** $3 : 4$
   **e** $3 : 2$   **f** $2 : 5$   **g** $2 : 3$

**6 a** $1 : 4$   **b** $2 : 1$   **c** $3 : 2$

**7 a** $2 : 1$   **b** $8 : 5$

**8 a** $1 : 10$   **b** $4 : 1$

**9 a** true   **b** false   **c** true   **d** true

**10** $3 : 1$

**11** $3 : 2$

## 7.2 Dividing using a ratio

**1 a** 5   **b** 10   **c** $1 : 2$

**2 a** 30   **b** $3 : 1$

**3 a** 5   **b** 25

**4 a** 12   **b** 6

**5** $5 : 1$

**6 a** 8   **b** 30

**7 a** 50 g   **b** 20 g

## 7.3 Proportion

1 a 18 km     b 5 hours
2 a 42 hours     b 133 hours
3 a £9.40     b £329
4 a £28.75     b 40 litres
5 a 16 g     b 90 g     c 100 ml
6 a 640 cm     b 6.4 m
7 a 32     b 12.5
8 a $1.30     b $123.50
9 a 63     b 150

## 7.4 Ratios and fractions

1 a 15     b 20     c $\frac{3}{4}$
2 a 2 : 1     b $\frac{2}{3}$
3 a 8 and 24     b $\frac{1}{4}$
4 $\frac{2}{5}$
5 3 : 2
6 a 4 : 5     b $\frac{5}{9}$
7 a 3 : 4     b $\frac{3}{4}$     c $\frac{4}{3}$
8 a 7 : 3     b $\frac{3}{10}$     c $\frac{3}{7}$

## 7 Problem solving

1 a 20     b 30p     c £1.20     d 2 : 3
   e $\frac{2}{5}$     f 11p     g £1.10

   h 500 g bag costs £1.20 per 100 g and 380 g bag cost £1.10 per 100 g, so 380 g better value
2 a 16 km/l     b 960 km     c €15.84     d €22
   e £14.40     f 120 miles     g 10 miles/l
   h 45 miles/gallon

# ANSWERS TO CHAPTER 8: PERCENTAGES

## 8.1 One number as a percentage of another

1 a $\frac{14}{100}$     b $\frac{28}{100}$     c $\frac{35}{100}$     d $\frac{70}{100}$
2 a 41%     b 82%     c 88%     d 30%
3 a 15%     b 78%     c 3%
4 a 67%     b 44%     c 78%     d 43%
5 a 65%     b 14     c 35%
6 a 65%     b 20%

7 a 85%     b 15%
8 Ali 48%, Beth 32%, Carl 20%
9 a 79%     b 21%

## 8.2 Comparisons using percentages

1 72%, 66%, 65%
2 a 80%     b 70%     c maths
3 a 36
   b 40% of girls have a pet which is less than 45%
4 $\frac{1}{4}$ = 25%, $\frac{1}{3}$ = 33%, 25% < 30% < 33%
5 a Dan 12.5%, Alice 10%     b Alice
6 a 71%     b Betaville is 66% which is less than 71%
7 a 79%     b B is 84% which is greater than 79%

## 8.3 Percentage change

1 a 150     b 750
2 a 24 cm     b 16 cm
3 a £0.78     b £16.38 an hour
4 a £64     b £384
5 a 1960     b 3640
6 a £39     b £91
7

| Item | Original price | Reduction | Sale price |
|------|------|------|------|
| Chair | £240 | £60 | £180 |
| Table | £600 | £150 | £450 |
| Bed | £840 | £210 | £630 |
| Cupboard | £360 | £90 | £270 |

8 £12 000

## 8 Problem solving

1 a 66 ÷ 80 = 0.825 = 82.5%     b 70% and 68%
   c Test A; A is 70%, B is 45% and C is 58%
   d i 350     ii 64%
   e Ali 72%, Emily 64%, Fran 56.3% so only Ali gets a Distinction.
2 a 16%     b £500     c £812.50     d 44%     e £625

# ANSWERS TO CHAPTER 9: ANGLES AND POLYGONS

## 9.1 Points and lines

1 $a = 90°$     $b = 135°$     $c = 56°$
2 $a = 120°$     $b = 205°$     $c = 120°$
3 a 30°     b 150°

**4** They add up to 355°, not 360°

**5 a** vertically opposite    **b** alternate
   **c** corresponding

**6** $a = 75°$ $b = 105°$ $c = 155°$ $d = 155°$

## 9.2 Triangles

**1 a** 30°    **b** 35°    **c** 110°    **d** 20°

**2** 45°

**3** $x = 60°$, $y = 30°$

**4** Third angle is $180° - 64° - 52° = 64°$, so two angles are 64°, therefore isosceles.

**5** R = 57°, P = 66°

**6** $180° - 130° = 50°$; $50° ÷ 2 = 25°$; each angle is 25°

**7** $a = 60°$, $b = 75°$

## 9.3 Quadrilaterals and other polygons

**1** 360°

**2** $a = 115°$, $b = 75°$, $c = 45°$, $d = 215°$

**3 a** 70°    **b** 110°

**4 a** kite    **b** 85°    **c** 40°

**5 a** trapezium    **b** 108°    **c** 125°

**6 a** hexagon    **b** 720°

**7 a** pentagon    **b** 150°    **c** 540°

## 9.4 Shapes on coordinate axes

**1 a, b**

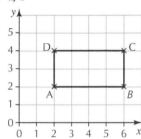

   **c** (2, 4)    **d** $x = 4$ and $y = 3$

**2 a, b, c**

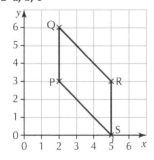

   **d** (5, 0)    **e** 45° and 135°

**3 a, b, c**

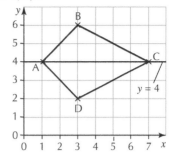

   **d** (3, 2)    **e** 90°

**4 a, b**

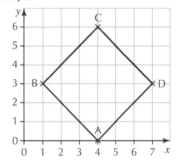

   **c** B(1, 3), D(7, 3)

**5 a, b**

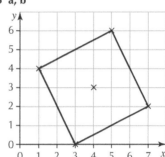

**6 a, b, c**

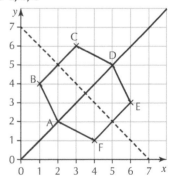

   **d** $x + y = 7$

## 9 Problem solving

**1 a**

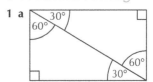

**b**

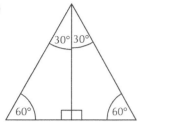

**c**

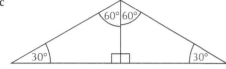

**d** 30°, 30° and 120°

**e**

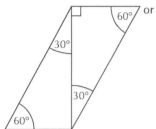

**f** 60°, 60°, 120° and 120° or 30°, 30°, 150° and 150°

**g**

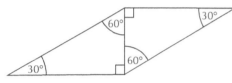

**h** 60°, 90°, 90° and 120°

**2 a** 3

**b** 3 angles = 360° so 1 angle = 360° ÷ 3 = 120°

**c** 4

**d** all 3 sides are the same length because they are sides of a regular hexagon.

**e** rhombus     **f** 60°, 60°, 120° and 120°

**g** 135°; rectangle angle + triangle angle = 90 + 45 = 135°

### 10.1 Perimeter and area

**1 a** 32 cm          **b** 26 cm
**2 a** 20 cm          **b** 22 m
**3 a** 21 cm²         **b** 30 m²
**4 a** 5 cm           **b** 25 cm²
**5 a** 50 cm²         **b** 25 cm²
**6 a** 14 cm²         **b** 24 m²
**7 a** 28 m           **b** 38 cm
**8 a** 40 m²          **b** 70 cm²
**9 a** 30 cm          **b** 42 cm²
**10 a** 30 cm         **b** 36 cm²

### 10.2 Circles

**1 a** chord          **b** tangent
**2 a** 16 cm          **b** 50 cm
**3** 63 cm
**4** 32 cm
**5 a** 75 cm   **b** 19 cm   **c** 53 cm   **d** 21 cm
**6** $\pi \times 5^2 = 79$ cm²
**7 a** 452 cm²   **b** 28 cm²   **c** 227 cm²   **d** 36 cm²
**8 a** 24 cm    **b** 88 cm²

### 10.3 Solids

**1 a** 6          **b** 12          **c** 8
**2 a** 5          **b** 9           **c** 6
**3 a** 20 cm²     **b** 12 cm²
**4** 32 cm²
**5 a** 9 cm²      **b** 63 cm³
**6 a** 180 cm³    **b** 288 cm³
**7 a i** 8     **ii** 18     **iii** 12     **b** 270 cm³
**8 a** 64 cm²     **b** 512 cm³

## 10 Problem solving

**1 a** 20 cm  **b** 24 cm²  **c** 28 cm  **d** 48 cm²

**e**

| T | T |
|---|---|

**f i** 32 cm  **ii** 48 cm²

**g** Possible answers include 3 cm by 8 cm **or** 2 cm by 12 cm **or** $1\frac{1}{2}$ cm by 16 cm **or** 1 cm by 24 cm

**h** Following on from part **g**, possible answers are 22 cm or 28 cm or 35 cm or 50 cm

**i** 25 cm²

**2 a** 9 cm²  **b** 54 cm²  **c** 27 cm³
**d** 36 cm  **e** 54 cm³  **f** 18 cm²
**g** 90 cm²  **h** 48 cm  **i** 144 cm

# ANSWERS TO CHAPTER 11: TRANSFORMATIONS

## 11.1 Reflections

**1 a**

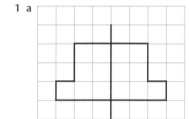

**b**

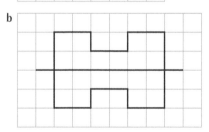

**2 a**

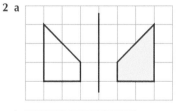

**b**

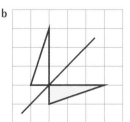

**3**

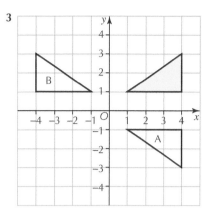

**4**

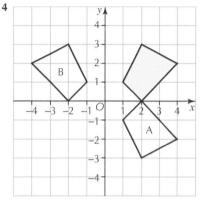

**5**

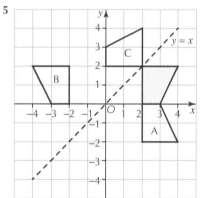

**6**

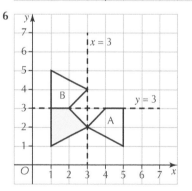

**7**

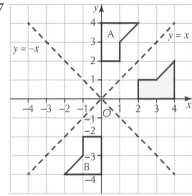

## 11.2 Translations and rotations

**1 a, b**

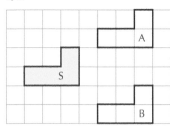

$$\mathbf{c}\begin{pmatrix}0\\4\end{pmatrix}$$

**2 a** $\begin{pmatrix}5\\3\end{pmatrix}$ **b** $\begin{pmatrix}-5\\0\end{pmatrix}$ **c** $\begin{pmatrix}5\\-3\end{pmatrix}$

**3**

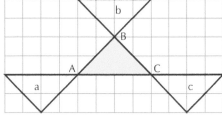

**4**

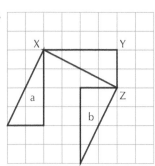

**5**

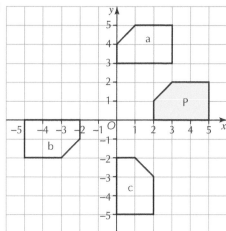

**6**

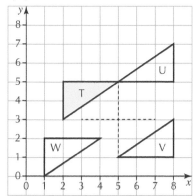

**7 a, b, d**

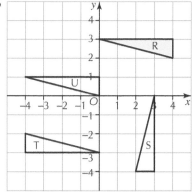

$$\mathbf{c}\begin{pmatrix}0\\-4\end{pmatrix}$$

## 11.3 Enlargements

**1 a** 3     **b** 18 cm

**2 a** 4     **b** 48 cm

**3** 180 cm

**4**

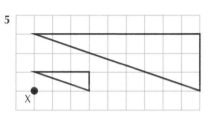

**5**

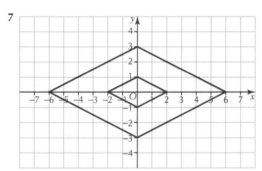

**6**

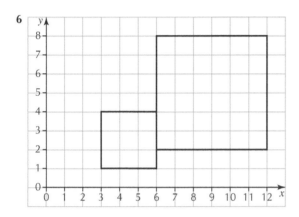

**7**

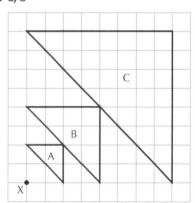

**8**

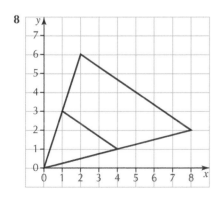

## 11 Problem solving

**1 a – f, h**

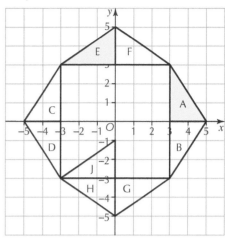

**g** rotation 90° clockwise, centre (0, 0)

**i** Reflection in the line $y = -3$

**2 a, b**

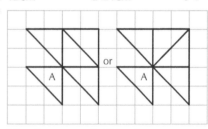

**c** 12 cm          **d** 24 cm          **e** 4

**f**

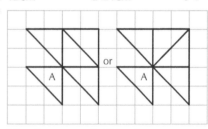

**g** 36 cm²          **h** 144 cm²

## ANSWERS TO CHAPTER 12: PROBABILITY

### 12.1 Relative frequency

**1 a** $\dfrac{13}{20}$          **b** $\dfrac{7}{20}$

**2 a** $\dfrac{9}{50}$          **b** $\dfrac{23}{50}$

**3 a** 200    **b i** 77%    **ii** 7%     **iii** 93%

**4 a** The frequencies for 4, 5, 6 are 2, 5, 2
   **b i** 0.2    **ii** 0.1    **iii** 0.6

**5 a** $\frac{573}{1000}$ or 0.573 or 57.3%     **b** 40

**6 a** $\frac{120}{200}$ or $\frac{3}{5}$ or 0.6 or 60%     **b** $\frac{20}{120}$ or $\frac{1}{6}$

   **c** $\frac{20}{32}$ or $\frac{5}{8}$ or 0.625 or 62.5%

## 12.2 Calculating probabilities

**1**

**2 a** $\frac{1}{6}$    **b** $\frac{2}{3}$    **c** $\frac{1}{2}$

**3 a** $\frac{3}{5}$    **b** $\frac{2}{5}$    **c** $\frac{9}{10}$

**4 a i** $\frac{2}{5}$   **ii** $\frac{1}{2}$   **iii** $\frac{9}{10}$   **b i** $\frac{4}{9}$   **ii** $\frac{5}{9}$   **iii** 1

**5 a** $\frac{2}{3}$    **b** $\frac{1}{3}$    **c** $\frac{1}{6}$

**6** 6

**7 a i** $\frac{1}{5}$   **ii** $\frac{12}{25}$   **iii** $\frac{8}{25}$   **b** 24

## 12.3 Possibility spaces

**1 a** AY, BX, BY, CX, CY    **b** AX, AY, AZ, CX, CY, CZ

**2 a**

| 1H | 2H | 3H | 4H | 5H | 6H |
|---|---|---|---|---|---|
| 1T | 2T | 3T | 4T | 5T | 6T |

   **b** 12    **c i** $\frac{1}{12}$    **ii** $\frac{3}{12} = \frac{1}{4}$

**3 a**

| RR | YR | BR |
|---|---|---|
| RY | YY | BY |
| RB | YB | BB |

   **b** 9    **c i** $\frac{1}{9}$    **ii** $\frac{3}{9} = \frac{1}{3}$    **iii** $\frac{6}{9} = \frac{2}{3}$

**4 a** 36    **b** $\frac{6}{36} = \frac{1}{6}$

   **c i** $\frac{1}{36}$   **ii** $\frac{6}{36} = \frac{1}{6}$   **iii** $\frac{9}{36} = \frac{1}{4}$   **iv** $\frac{11}{36}$

**5 a**

| 7 | 8 | 9 | 10 | 11 | 12 |
|---|---|---|---|---|---|
| 6 | 7 | 8 | 9 | 10 | 11 |
| 5 | 6 | 7 | 8 | 9 | 10 |
| 4 | 5 | 6 | 7 | 8 | 9 |
| 3 | 4 | 5 | 6 | 7 | 8 |
| 2 | 3 | 4 | 5 | 6 | 7 |

   **b** 7    **c** 2 or 12

   **d i** $\frac{1}{36}$   **ii** $\frac{2}{36} = \frac{1}{18}$   **iii** $\frac{5}{36}$   **iv** $\frac{6}{36} = \frac{1}{6}$

## 12 Problem solving

**1 a i** 0.3    **ii** 0.15    **iii** 0.55

   **b**

| Green | Yellow | Red | Total |
|---|---|---|---|
| 13 | 9 | 28 | 50 |

   **c i** 0.26    **ii** 0.18    **iii** 0.56
   **d i** 0.2    **ii** 0.2    **iii** 0.6

   **e** No. They do not have to be exactly the same. They are quite similar. No convincing evidence it is unfair.

**2 a**

| HH | TH |
|---|---|
| HT | TT |

   **b i** $\frac{1}{4}$    **ii** $\frac{1}{2}$

   **c**

| HHH | HTH | THH | TTH |
|---|---|---|---|
| HHT | HTT | THT | TTT |

   **d i** $\frac{1}{8}$    **ii** $\frac{3}{8}$    **iii** $\frac{3}{8}$

   **e** This is a possible answer. The order of the columns could be different.

**Coins 1, 2 and 3**

| | | HHH | HHT | HTH | HTT | THH | THT | TTH | TTT |
|---|---|---|---|---|---|---|---|---|---|
| **Coin 4** | **Head (H)** | HHHH | HHTH | HTHH | HTTH | THHH | THTH | TTHH | TTTH |
| | **Tail (T)** | HHHT | HHTT | HTHT | HTTT | THHT | THTT | TTHT | TTTT |

   **f i** $\frac{1}{16}$    **ii** $\frac{4}{16} = \frac{1}{4}$    **iii** $\frac{6}{16} = \frac{3}{8}$

# ANSWERS TO CHAPTER 13: STATISTICS

## 13.1 Tables, charts and diagrams

**1 a** B     **b** C     **c** £54

**2 a** 25

**b**

**Telephone calls to helpline**

Monday

Tuesday

Wednesday

**3 a** Belgium     **b** 6 million     **c** 48 million

**4 a** January and February     **b** May     **c** 7

**5 a** 9     **b** 4     **c** 5

## 13.2 Calculating statistics

**1 a** football     **b** rugby

**2 a** 17 years     **b** 15 years     **c** 9 years

**3 a i** £9.30    **ii** £6.30    **b i** £10.15    **ii** £6.30

**4 a**

| 3 | 4 | 5 | 6 | 7 |
|---|---|---|---|---|
| 7 | 2 | 3 | 0 | 1 |

  **b i** 1    **ii** 2    **iii** 7

**5 a** 8 minutes     **b** 4.8 minutes

**6 a** 23     **b** 37     **c** 32

**7 a i** 6 hours    **ii** 4 hours    **iii** 5 hours

  **b** 21 hours

## 13 Problem solving

**1 a** 1900 Kj     **b** Crispbread     **c** 300 Kj

**d**

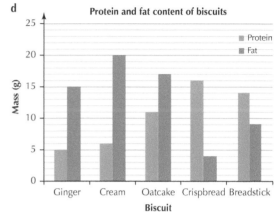

**e** 11 g     **f** 16 g     **g i** C    **ii** E    **iii** B

**2 a** 14 minutes     **b** 9 minutes     **c** 19 minutes

  **d** 17 minutes

**e**

| 8 | 9 | 10 | 11 | 12 | 13 | 14 |
|---|---|----|----|----|----|----|
| 6 | 5 | 2 | 6 | 5 | 5 | 11 |

**f i** 6 minutes    **ii** 14 minutes    **iii** 12 minutes

**g** 11.45 minutes

**h** Task 5. The mean time is 8.75 minutes, which is 2.7 minutes less than task 4.